THE
GOSPEL
FOR
TODAY

Register This New Book

Benefits of Registering*

- ✓ FREE **replacements** of lost or damaged books
- ✓ FREE **audiobook** – *Pilgrim's Progress*, audiobook edition
- ✓ FREE information about new titles and other **freebies**

www.anekopress.com/new-book-registration

*See our website for requirements and limitations.

THE GOSPEL FOR TODAY

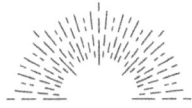

New Evangelistic Sermons
FOR A NEW DAY

Reuben A. Torrey

We love hearing from our readers. Please contact us
at www.anekopress.com/questions-comments with
any questions, comments, or suggestions.

The Gospel for Today
© 2022 by Aneko Press
All rights reserved. First edition 1922.
Revisions copyright 2022.

Please do not reproduce, store in a retrieval system, or transmit in any form or by any means – electronic, mechanical, photocopying, recording, or otherwise, without written permission from the publisher. Please contact us via www.AnekoPress.com for reprint and translation permissions.

Scripture quotations from The Authorized (King James) Version. Rights in the Authorized Version in the United Kingdom are vested in the Crown. Reproduced by permission of the Crown's patentee, Cambridge University Press.

Cover Designer: J. Martin, Jonathan Lewis
Editors: Sheila Wilkinson, Ruth Clark

Aneko Press
www.anekopress.com
Aneko Press, Life Sentence Publishing, and our logos are trademarks of
Life Sentence Publishing, Inc.
203 E. Birch Street
P.O. Box 652
Abbotsford, WI 54405

RELIGION / Christianity / General
Paperback ISBN: 978-1-62245-731-1
eBook ISBN: 978-1-62245-732-8
10 9 8 7 6 5 4 3 2 1
Available where books are sold

Contents

Preface vii

Ch. 1: A Converted Unbeliever's Preaching 1

Ch. 2: The Keynote of the Bible 15

Ch. 3: The Most Wonderful Sentence Ever Written 31

Ch. 4: The Only Gospel That Has Saving Power 49

Ch. 5: The Great Attraction: The Uplifted Christ 63

Ch. 6: The Most Important Question of the Day 77

Ch. 7: Great Things and How Anyone Can Get Them 91

Ch. 8: Noah and the Ark 105

Ch. 9: Time and Eternity Contrasted 121

Ch. 10: Eternal Life or the Wrath of God: Which Will You Choose? 131

Ch. 11: A Perfect Cure for Poverty and All Other Evils of the Day 145

Ch. 12: Jesus Is the Christ, the Son of God 161

Ch. 13: Which Shall We Believe: God or Man? 175

Reuben A. Torrey – A Brief Biography 189

Other Similar Titles 191

Preface

Repeated and insistent demands for more evangelistic sermons have come to me from pastors, evangelists, and publishers. I have felt the force of these demands and at last am yielding to them by publishing this new volume of sermons.

For the most part, I preached these sermons to my own congregation in Los Angeles in the past few months, and in His wondrous grace, God has seen fit to bless them. He used them for the conversion of a good many persons, the great majority of whom have been men from the ages of twenty-five to fifty, but there have been some men of riper years converted, even up to seventy or eighty years of age. There have also been some notable conversions among women. We have been greatly interested in the number of Jews and Roman Catholics who have recently made a public profession of accepting Christ in our after-meetings, many of whom have then united with our church, the Church of the Open Door. Not a few of those converted were former skeptics, agnostics, infidels, and atheists, and quite a number of Christian Scientists.

The gospel presented in these sermons is the same gospel of a crucified Christ, a Savior from the guilt of sin, and a risen Christ, a Savior from the present power of sin, that we have been preaching throughout our entire ministry as pastor and as evangelist in all parts of the world. Yet we are certainly living in a new day. The war (World War I) and its aftermath have worked a radical transformation in the ethical and religious as well as the social and economic outlooks in the minds of the men and women of the present day. Nevertheless, we find that the same gospel that was *the power of God unto salvation* before the war and from the days of the apostle Paul (Romans 1:16), is the gospel that men will listen to and yield to today. All of these new gospels, the "social gospel," and the rest, are proving utterly ineffective in saving individual men or in lifting up communities. When preached in the power of the Holy Spirit, the real gospel produces the same effects in individual lives today and in the transformation of families and communities that it produced throughout all the centuries since our Lord Jesus Christ died on the cross of Calvary, rose again, and ascended to the right hand of the Father. He then poured out His Holy Spirit upon His people. Practical results prove that the real gospel does not need to be restated; of course, it is desirable to adapt the illustrations and method of argument to the thinking of our own day.

There seems to be a great religious awakening in Scotland and in some parts of Ireland and England, and there are indications here and there of an awakening in our own land. It cannot be denied that many pastors who are thoroughly evangelical and many of our most intelligent laymen are tired of some of the methods of evangelism that have been in vogue in our own country during the past few years. This does not mean for one moment that they do not believe in evangelism or in true revivals.

We seem to be ripe for a revival now, and it is hoped that these sermons may prove helpful in promoting that greatly longed-for and earnestly prayed-for genuine revival. We hope they may be helpful to pastors in their desire to become their own evangelists and to those evangelists whom God has chosen. We hope that they may be directly used for the salvation of many souls by being put in the hands of men, women, and children who are unsaved and need a Savior. It has been a great joy to this author to receive letters from different parts of the world, from all classes of people, saying that they had been led to Christ through reading printed reports of his sermons.

In our own church, we have found that it has not been necessary to introduce movies or other sensational features to draw the crowds. We have never had a movie or anything of that kind in our church and never expect to have them. And yet our Sunday-evening audiences at which these sermons were preached were probably larger than those of any other church in the community, even those resorting to the movies as a means of drawing a crowd. In fact, we think there is no other building used for religious services in the city that would hold the thousands of people who have listened to these sermons Sunday night after Sunday night. What the great attraction is that brings men and women to the house of God, as well as brings them to a better life, is stated in the fifth sermon in this book.

Reuben A. Torrey
Los Angeles, CA

Chapter 1

A Converted Unbeliever's Preaching

And straightway he preached Christ in the synagogues, that he is the Son of God. (Acts 9:20)

You will find the text in Acts 9:20: *And straightway he preached Christ in the synagogues, that he is the Son of God.* The Revised Version is even more suggestive: *And straightway in the synagogues he proclaimed Jesus, that he is the Son of God.* Perhaps there was never a more amazed audience than the one that heard Saul of Tarsus preach his first sermon in Damascus. Saul was known far and wide as a hater of Jesus Christ and as a persecutor of Christians. He had come to Damascus for the express purpose of destroying the church, arresting all believers in Jesus Christ, and dragging them to Jerusalem for punishment and death. It is unlikely that there is so bitter an infidel alive today as Saul of Tarsus, and yet in his first public appearance in Damascus, this same Saul of Tarsus preaches a sermon of tremendous power, declaring and proving that Jesus is the Son of God. If you consider two things earnestly and honestly, they may result in some of you being converted. The first thing to look at is the preacher in the text, and the second thing is the preacher's message.

The Preacher

Look first at the preacher. The preacher was Saul of Tarsus. As you look at him, I wish to submit three good reasons why this particular preacher's message should command attention and should be accepted. Taken together, these three reasons prove that the message is undoubtedly true.

Initially, he had been a hater of the Jesus whom he now proclaimed. Saul had not been brought up to believe that Jesus was the Son of God, and therefore he did not preach it because it was what he had been taught to believe from childhood. There are many who say of our modern preachers, "Oh, he believes that and preaches that just because it is what his parents and early teachers taught him to believe." But no such charge can be brought against Saul of Tarsus. The doctrine that Jesus was the Son of God was not something Saul had taken up without any due thought, not something that he had inherited from his parents and early teachers.

Saul had opposed this doctrine with all the vigor of an intense soul. He had gone up and down the streets of the city of Jerusalem, in and out of the houses, arresting men, women, and children for no other reason than that they believed that Jesus was the Son of God and confessed their faith in Him as such. He had attended their trials and voted for their death. Nothing seemed to cause him greater joy than the violent death of some Christian. He had taken part in the murder of the first Christian martyr, Stephen.

Not only that, but when he had exhausted all his opportunities of demonstrating his hatred of Christians in Jerusalem in violent ways, his hatred of Christ and Christianity was not satisfied, and he sought and obtained authority to go to Damascus to carry out a similar work of opposition and destruction there. Now when a man like that turns completely around and says, "I was wrong; I was utterly wrong; I was awfully wrong in my denial that Jesus was the Son of God," then we ought to give his change of opinion careful attention. He must have had some good reason for it.

In addition to that, he sacrificed for his testimony and change of opinion. Saul's change of opinion cost him much, so his witness should carry great weight. It cost him everything of a worldly character that he possessed. It cost him the loss of a position of great influence and promise and the loss of all his old friends. It cost him the severest persecution: arrest after arrest, imprisonment after imprisonment, scourging after scourging, stoning and insults, and attempted assassination. It cost him wandering and hunger and nakedness; it cost him suffering of the most intense kind and dangers of indescribable magnitude. When a man of standing and education like Saul of Tarsus makes sacrifices like that for a change of opinion, his new opinion must demand great consideration.

Of course, men are constantly changing their opinions because they are going to gain something by the change. Many a Republican becomes a Democrat, and many a Democrat becomes a Republican because of some personal profit that is to come to them in one way or another from the change. Of course, a change of opinion in a case like that is not worthy of much consideration.

Some professed Christians have become infidels, outspoken infidels, because they could make money by the change or because they had sinned. The truth of Christianity caused them shame, and they wished to clear their consciences, or they desired to gain some other low end by the change of opinion.

When I was in Sydney, Australia, a man was urged to come

and hear my address, but he replied that he took no stock in that sort of thing, that he had been a preacher and a missionary once and had found the whole thing was a humbug. I took the time to look into the man's history and I found that his change of opinion was not due to further information and study that had shown him that Christianity was untrue. Instead, once a missionary, he had gotten into trouble for his immorality and he was expelled from the mission, as he should have been. In that way he was led to change his opinion about Christianity and to accept infidelity. But when a man of great intelligence changes his opinion, sacrifices everything that men hold dear for that change, and is transformed in character by the change, then one should look closely at what caused the change. When the man who changes is a man like Saul of Tarsus who became Paul the apostle, any honest man will hesitate a long time before he says Saul was mistaken in the change.

> When a man changes his opinion, and is transformed in character by the change, then one should look closely at what caused the change.

But there is another reason, and a better one yet, why Saul's opinion must carry great weight. Indeed, it is so absolutely conclusive that if we are thoroughly honest, we must say that Saul was certainly right in what he says, and that Jesus is as Saul said He was, the Son of God. Why did Saul change from the opinion that Jesus was an impostor and a blasphemer to the opinion that Jesus was the Son of God? Saul himself tells us why he changed his opinion. He says it was because as he drew near to Damascus to arrest the Christians and bring them to Jerusalem to be punished, at the noon hour there suddenly shone around him a great light from heaven. Above the light of the noontime sun and in that light he saw the face and form of Jesus who was once crucified, but now risen and glorified. He *heard a voice saying unto [him], Saul, Saul, why persecutest thou me?* And when he inquired who was speaking to him, the form there in the glory said, *I am Jesus of Nazareth, whom thou persecutest* (Acts 22:6-8, 16-18; cf. 9:5-6).

Now, if Saul of Tarsus really saw Jesus in the glory, and if Jesus said to Saul what Saul reports that He said, and if Saul was commissioned at that time, as he said he was, to be the authoritative representative of this same Jesus, then Jesus certainly is the Son of God. There remains no room for debate about that. But the question arises, did Saul really see Jesus in this way and hear Him say the things he said He did? Either he did or Saul was a liar and made the story up, or he was mistaken and had a sunstroke or something of that sort that he imagined it was a reality.

Did he lie and make the story up? Such a supposition is incredible. There was no reason for the lie; there was nothing to be gained by the lie; there was everything to be lost by it. Men do not manufacture lies for the sake of sacrificing position, home, money, comfort, ease, reputation, love of friends, and everything dear to them in life. The supposition, then, that Saul of Tarsus lied in this matter is ruled out. Was Paul the victim of delusion and fabrication through sunstroke or a flash of lightning and a peal of thunder (which he mistook for the voice of Jesus) or overwrought imagination, or something of that kind, so that he imagined that he saw something he did not see and heard something he did not hear?

To this we would say that the record and well-attested facts in the case make this explanation impossible. Not only did Saul see the light, but those who journeyed with him also saw the light, so it could not have been Paul's imagination. And not only did those who journeyed with him see the light, they also heard the voice, though they did not distinguish the message that was spoken. Furthermore, Paul was blind for three days, and that was no delusion.

There was also another man, Ananias, who saw Jesus in a vision, and this Jesus whom he saw in the vision said, *Arise, and go to the street which is called Straight, and inquire in the house of Judas for one named Saul, a man of Tarsus: for behold, he prayeth; and he hath seen a man named Ananias coming in, and laying his hands on him, that he might receive his sight* (Acts 9:11-12). Ananias protested against going, saying, *Lord, I have heard from many of this man, how much evil he did to thy saints at Jerusalem: and here he hath authority from the chief priests to bind all that call upon thy name* (Acts 9:13-14). But the Lord who appeared to him in the vision insisted upon his going, and he obeyed. He found Saul where the Lord Jesus had told him in the vision he would find him, and he *entered into the house; and laying his hands on him said, Brother Saul, the Lord, even Jesus, who appeared unto thee in the way which thou camest, hath sent me, that thou mayest receive thy sight, and be filled with the Holy Ghost* (Acts 9:17).

And immediately there fell from Saul's eyes the scales, and he received his sight. There is absolutely no room for the theory of delusion and imagination on Paul's part here. Did someone say the whole story in Acts is fictional? Let them study it. I challenge any honest lawyer or historical critic to study this story carefully and candidly with the desire to find out whether it is truth or fiction; see if this story does not bear the unmistakable marks of truth.

In the eighteenth century, rationalism had swept away everything before it in England. There were very few, even among the clergy, who still believed in the supernatural, but there were some remains of faith in the miracles and the historical accuracy of the Bible, so the rationalists of the day appointed two of their ablest reasoners to undertake a campaign for the destruction of what remained of faith in the supernatural. They selected Lord Lyttelton, an able lawyer, and Sir Gilbert West, clerk of the Privy Council. These two men planned a campaign for the destruction of belief in the supernatural. One of them said to the other, "If we are to destroy faith in the supernatural, there are two alleged incidents in the Bible that we must prove to be legend or myth. One is the alleged resurrection of Jesus Christ from the dead, and the other is the alleged conversion of Saul of Tarsus."

Lord Lyttelton said to Sir Gilbert West, "Well, I will take the story of the conversion of Saul of Tarsus as recorded in the Acts of the Apostles and show it is not historical fact but legend." And Sir Gilbert West replied that he would take the story of the alleged resurrection of Jesus Christ and show that it was not historical fact but legend or myth.

Then West turned to Lyttelton and said, "I will depend upon you for my Bible material, for I must confess that I am somewhat rusty in the Bible."

Lyttelton replied, "I was intending to depend upon you for my biblical material, for I also am somewhat rusty in the Bible." Then one of them said, "Well, we must be candid and carefully study the records in the Bible." They met a number of times while they were preparing their books. On one of these occasions, Lyttelton said, "West, as I have been studying the record in the Bible, I have become somewhat shaken in my position."

West replied, "Well, I am glad to hear you say it, for I confess that as I have been studying the records regarding the resurrection of Christ, I have become somewhat shaken in *my* position." But they went on and completed their books.

At a last conference, West said to Lyttelton, "Have you written your book?"

He replied, "Yes, I have, but as I have studied the facts as presented in the Bible and applied the canons of evidence received in courts of law to them, I have become satisfied of the truth of the Bible record. Saul of Tarsus was converted just as it is recorded in the ninth chapter of the Acts of the Apostles." Then he added, "Have you written your book?"

"Yes," Sir Gilbert West replied, "I have written my book, but as I have sifted the evidence regarding the resurrection of Jesus Christ as found in the Bible, I have become satisfied that Jesus Christ *did* rise from the dead, just as recorded in the Gospels, and I have written my book on that side."

Anyone who will do what this gifted lawyer did and sit down to a careful study of the conversion of Saul of Tarsus as related in three different places in the Acts of the Apostles, and as referred to in the Epistles, with an honest desire to know whether it is truth or fiction will be compelled to come to the same conclusion that Lord Lyttelton did.

We arrive then at this point – that Saul of Tarsus changed from a bitter infidel to a believer in Jesus Christ, and preached that "Jesus is the Son of God" because Jesus Christ appeared to him in glory as the Son of God. Saul of Tarsus actually saw him, and Jesus Christ appointed Saul as His authoritative representative. It has been absolutely settled, not as a theological speculation, but as an established historical fact established by conclusive testimony and evidence, that Jesus is the Son of God.

> It has been absolutely settled, established by conclusive testimony and evidence, that Jesus is the Son of God.

The Converted Infidel's Message

We can now turn from a consideration of the preacher to a consideration of the preacher's message. What was the preacher's message? What was the message this converted infidel brought to the people of Damascus and brings to us today? His message can be summed up in one short sentence: Jesus is the Son of God.

Look at Saul as he stands there and proclaims it. He stands

there as a man who a few days before had been a bitter hater of Jesus Christ and Christianity. He was a man who had stained his hands with Christian blood, a man who had come to Damascus for the express purpose of arresting men and women because they believed in Jesus of Nazareth as the Christ, the Son of God, and professed their faith in Him. Around him stood Jews and others who had heard of him as the bitterest enemy that the cause of Jesus Christ had, and as a man who stopped at nothing in his efforts to stamp out Christianity. To their amazement, he declares to them that upon indisputable testimony he had found this Jesus, whom he had persecuted, to be the Son of God. But God Himself stands in this audience, proclaiming this same message. Let us look closely at this message.

Note first that the message is not that Jesus is a good man or even the best man that ever lived on this earth; no, the message is that JESUS IS THE SON OF GOD. That is, He is a man who stands absolutely apart from all other men, and while He is a man, He is more than a man. He is of divine origin, partakes of all the attributes of the Deity, and is to be honored and worshipped even as God the Father is honored and worshipped.

And secondly, note that the message is not merely that Jesus is a great teacher, but that Jesus is also the Son of God. Then notice that the message is not only that Jesus is a perfect man and our example, but that Jesus is also the Son of God.

Jesus Is the Son of God. What Does That Involve?

Absolute Trust

First of all, it involves absolute and wholehearted trust in Him. If Jesus is the Son of God, then I can trust Him absolutely and wholeheartedly. I cannot trust any man absolutely and wholeheartedly, no matter how good he may be. I could not absolutely and wholeheartedly trust any man. The Word of God is right when it says, *Thus saith the* LORD; *Cursed be the man that trusteth in man* (Jeremiah 17:5). If Jesus is not merely a man, if He is divine, if He is the Son of God, if He is God manifest in human form, then I can trust Him absolutely, and that is what He demands that I should do.

On the night before His crucifixion, Jesus demanded of His disciples the same absolute trust in Himself that they put in God the Father. He said, *Let not your heart be troubled: ye believe in God, believe also in me* (John 14:1). As He is the Son of God, He had a right to make the demand that men should put their absolute trust in Him. If He had been merely a man, even the best of men, He would not have demanded that these men bring the curse of God upon their heads by putting their absolute trust in Him. But because He was the Son of God and because He was God manifest in the flesh, He could say, *Believe in God, believe also in me.* And that is what He is saying to each of us; that is what He is demanding of us.

Salvation from Sin

Next, believing that Jesus is the Son of God also involves that we not only trust Him absolutely and wholeheartedly in a general way, but that we also trust Him specifically for salvation – salvation from the guilt of sin and salvation from the power of sin. No matter how utterly lost we may be, no matter how many sins we may have committed, no matter how completely we may be in the power of sin right now, Jesus is the Son of God, and according to His own Word, He died upon the cross of Calvary in our stead. As the Son of God, He could make a perfect atonement for sin, and the moment we trust in Him, our sins are all forgiven.

Furthermore, as He is the Son of God, He has power to save us from the power of sin. Sin may be stronger than we are; Satan may be stronger than we are; they are both strong, but they are not as strong as the Son of God, and this Son of God undertakes to save all from the power of sin who put their trust in Him. He also said, *If therefore the Son shall make you free, ye shall be free indeed* (John 8:36). As the Son of God He has power to set free from the power of sin anyone who puts their trust in Him.

Surrender

In addition to being saved from the power of sin, a real faith that Jesus is the Son of God involves the surrender of our life to Him. If Jesus is divine, if He is the Son of God, if He is God made manifest in the flesh, then we should surrender to Him all that we are and all that we have. That is what He demands of us and has a right to demand of us.

Remember, Jesus is the Son of God! Have you made a surrender of your whole life to Him? If not, will you make that surrender now?

Real belief that Jesus is the Son of God also involves the surrender of our thoughts to Him. If Jesus is the Son of God, He is infallible; He can never be mistaken. Therefore, if some man, no matter how learned he may be, no matter how high he may stand in circles of education and culture, says one thing, and Jesus, the Son of God, says another, then no man who really believes that Jesus is the Son of God will hesitate one moment which to believe.

I have surrendered my thoughts absolutely to the shaping and to the control of Jesus Christ, for I am convinced, I am absolutely sure, that He is the Son of God, and I say to any man, "Do you dare to set up your poor miserable opinions against the plain declarations of the Son of God? If you do, you are a fool, and however much you may resent the statement, the day is coming when you will see that you are a fool. God grant that it may not come when it is too late to repent." There is saving power in this doctrine that Jesus is the Son of God. It will save any man who believes it from the heart and acts upon it.

This doctrine will bring eternal life to anyone who believes it, really believes it from the heart, and shows that he believes it by acting upon it. The apostle John says in John 20:31, *These are written* [that is, these things written in the Gospel of John], *that ye might believe that Jesus is the Christ, the Son of God; and that believing ye might have life through his name.* We see here that through simply believing that Jesus is the Christ, the Son of God, believing it with the heart, anyone who thus believes obtains eternal life.

Believing in this doctrine will also bring victory over the world. In his first epistle John says, *Who is he that overcometh the world, but he that believeth that Jesus is the Son of God?* (1 John 5:5). The world has a mighty power, a power to blind our minds, a power to break our resolutions, a power to degrade our lives. The great masses of men and women are yielding to this power of the world; they are giving up their high ideals and compromising with things that their own consciences condemn – things that are low and debasing. The world, the spirit of the times, the ideas that rule in this world which *lieth in the evil one* (1 John 5:19) are making a mighty assault on the faith and moral principles and the conduct of us all. That assault is too strong for any of us to resist in our own strength, but there is a way of victory – by believing, really believing, that Jesus is the Son of God.

> There is a way of victory – by believing, really believing, that Jesus is the Son of God.

I believe that practically everyone in this audience is convinced that Jesus is the Son of God, but being intellectually convinced of a thing is one thing, and really believing it from the heart and yielding our will to that which our mind accepts is quite another thing. Today, will you accept Jesus Christ as the Son of God? Will you take that attitude toward Him that you ought to take toward one that you know to be the Son of God? Will you from this time on trust Him absolutely? Will you trust Him through His atoning death for the pardon of all your sins? Will you trust Him daily for His divine power for deliverance from the power of sin? Will you surrender your life absolutely to Him? Will you surrender your thoughts to Him for Him to be absolute ruler of your thoughts? It is up to each one of you to answer the question. You can say yes or no, whichever you want. Which will you say?

Chapter 2

The Keynote of the Bible

God is love. (1 John 4:8)

Our subject is "The Keynote of the Bible."
You will find the keynote of the Bible in my text – 1 John 4:8, *God is love.* That is one of the shortest sentences ever written, and it is certainly one of the greatest and most profound. It is inexhaustible in its meaning and scope. Men have been studying, scrutinizing, pondering, and digging into that sentence throughout the eighteen centuries that have passed since it was written, and they have not exhausted it yet. Thousands upon thousands of sermons have been preached upon that text, yet something new awaits every preacher who studies it and seeks to expound upon it. Thousands of volumes have been written by some of the world's greatest thinkers devoted to the study, exposition, and application of that sentence, but it is as fresh and full as ever. It is constantly yielding new treasures to each new century and to each new explorer of its exhaustless wealth. Men and angels will ponder that sentence throughout the endless ages of eternity and not exhaust it.

The Book that contains that matchless sentence bears the unmistakable seal of having God for its Author. The golden truth of priceless worth contained in this sentence is peculiar to the Bible. All the philosophers in the world never discovered that astounding truth until God revealed it and the Bible declared it. The world would never have known that *God is love* had God not revealed the fact in His own Word. It is true that there are evidences of benevolent design in nature and in history, but nature and history have both been marred by Satan's work and by the entrance of sin into the world. It is only that interpretation of history and that insight into the future of man, nature, and Satan that the Bible gives that enables us to see love reigning above all and through all.

We hear much today of the profound truths contained in the teachings of the world's great philosophers of ancient and modern times, in philosophers like Socrates, Plato, Aristotle, Seneca, Isocrates, Epictetus, Marcus Aurelius Antoninus, and in the teachings of the great founders of religions like Buddha, Muhammad, Confucius, and Zoroaster. But in none of them do we find this great truth that *God is love* or anything like it, not until the Bible revealed it. We owe this truth wholly and solely to the Bible. We must go then to the Bible for the interpretation of this truth.

> The Bible is one great, ever-swelling anthem, and the theme of that anthem is God is love.

This sentence is the keynote of the entire Bible. It is the great fundamental thought of the Bible. If anyone were to ask me to put into one sentence what the Bible teaches, I could do it. And this would be the sentence: *God is love.* From start to finish, from Genesis 1:1 to Revelation 22:21, the Bible is one great, ever-swelling anthem, and the theme of that anthem is *God is love.* God's love is the keynote of the whole Bible, of each one of the sixty-six books that go to make up the completed whole.

The love of God led to the creation as described in the first chapter of Genesis. God's love led to the banishment of Adam and Eve from the garden of Eden when they fell, as recorded in the third chapter of Genesis. God's love led to the promise of the Savior, the seed of the woman, immediately after Adam and Eve had fallen. God's love led to the call of Abraham and Jacob to be a blessing first to their own descendants and ultimately to the whole human race. God's love led to the bondage of Israel in Egypt and to their deliverance from that bondage when the time was ripe. God's love led to the giving of the law through Moses on Sinai, and God's love led to the extermination of the Canaanites.

It was God's love that led to the planting of Israel in that land so wondrously adapted by its natural configuration and by its location in the then-inhabited world, to be the training place of the nation that would bring blessing to the whole earth and from which the Savior would be born. God's love shaped Israel's history through all their wanderings from Him. And God's love at last rooted Israel out of the land He had given them and scattered them throughout the earth.

Then God's love will restore them again to the land that belongs to them by eternal covenant when the time is full. God's love sent Jesus Christ to die for sinful men, to rise again from the dead, and to ascend to the right hand of the Father in glory. And it will be God's love that will send Him back to earth when the fullness of time for that greatest event in all this earth's history has come. Heaven and all its glories, hell and all its horrors both have their origin in the love of God. Yes, *God is love* is the keynote of the Bible, the secret of history, the explanation of nature, and the solution of eternity's mysteries.

I wish to call your attention to some of the ways in which the love of God is manifested. Of course, it would take many sermons to recount all the manifestations of the love of God, but we can look at some of them, even though it would take all eternity to fully understand and appreciate even them.

God's Love Is Manifested in His Provisions for Us

In the first place, God's love manifests itself in His ministering to all our needs and to our fullest joy. This comes out again and again in the Bible. Our Lord Jesus expounded to His disciples their duty when He said, *Love your enemies, and pray for them that persecute you; that ye may be sons of your Father which is in heaven: for he maketh his sun to rise on the evil and the good, and sendeth rain on the just and the unjust* (Matthew 5:44-45). And way back in the Old Testament in Deuteronomy 32:9-12 we read: *For the LORD's portion is his people; Jacob is the lot of his inheritance. He found him in a desert land, and in the waste howling wilderness; he compassed him about, he cared for him, he kept him as the apple of his eye: as an eagle that stirreth up her nest, that fluttereth over her young, he spread abroad his wings, he took them, he bare them on his pinions: the LORD alone did lead him, and there was no strange god with him.*

This is a marvelous picture of the wondrous love of God. Every blessing of life is a love token from God. As the Holy Spirit puts it through the apostle James in James 1:17: *Every good gift and every perfect gift is from above, and cometh down from the Father of lights, with whom is no variableness, neither shadow of turning.*

When the sun shines with its warmth and light and gladness, lift up your head with joy and say, "This is a token of my Father's love." When you look upon the blossoming flowers, the growing grass, the budding trees in their spring beauty, say, "All this beauty with which God adorns the earth is another token of God's love for me." When you feel health and strength coursing through your veins, look up and thank God again, for this is another token of His love. The countless blessings that come to us every day of our lives, most of them unnoticed in our blindness and ingratitude, are all tokens of His great and constant love.

God's Love Chastens Us

In the second place, God's love for His children, even those who are not yet His children, is manifested in His chastening when we forget Him, wander from Him, and fall into sin. This is very clear in that beautiful passage, Hebrews 12:6-10:

For whom the Lord loveth he chasteneth, and scourgeth every son whom he receiveth. It is for chastening that ye endure; God dealeth with you as with sons; for what son is there whom his father chasteneth not? But if ye are without chastening, whereof all have been made partakers, then are ye bastards, and not sons. Furthermore, we had the fathers of our flesh to chasten us, and we gave them reverence: shall we not much rather be in subjection unto the Father of spirits, and live? For they verily for a few days chastened us as seemed good to them; but he for our profit, that we may be partakers of his holiness.

We see that God's love manifests itself in chastening us and in sending us trials and pain and bereavement and sorrow.

Many cannot see any proof of God's love in their many and great afflictions. It seems to them that God does not love them when He allows them to suffer such awful and sometimes such appalling griefs and trials, but those who think that are very blind. Don't we chasten our own beloved children? Don't we do it because we love them and for their good? It would often be easier for us not to do it. It would spare our feelings, for we suffer far more than they do when we punish them, if we are true parents. Some parents are so unloving and so self-centered that they allow their children to go unpunished in their folly and sin in order to spare their own feelings.

But not so with our heavenly Father. He really loves us, wisely loves us, and so chastens us for our highest good. Sometimes when our conduct makes it necessary, He very severely chastises us, or as the Bible puts it, He *scourges* us. Every wise man thanks God for His chastening love, even in its severest manifestations.

For twelve years or more God spared my wife and me and our family in our home life from serious sickness. We had gone through epidemics of many kinds unscathed. When threatened with croup, scarlet fever, typhoid fever, diphtheria, and other diseases, we cried to God and He gave deliverance again and again. But a day came when God permitted diphtheria to enter our home, and a few short hours after the real character of the disease was discovered, it took from us a beautiful child when we thought all danger of death was past. It was a stunning blow, just twenty-four years ago this week, and March 17 never comes around without our thinking of it. For the first time the family circle was broken. The body of our child had been carried from our happy home and laid in the lonely cemetery. Why did God permit that? Because He loved us. We needed it.

The following Sunday night I spoke on Hebrews 12:6: *For whom the Lord loveth he chasteneth, and scourgeth every son whom he receiveth.* This chastisement, yes, this scourging, led to deep heart-searchings and discovery of failure and thereby led to confession of sin. It led also to new consecration and love for souls and devotion to God. It brought the answer to prayers that had been ascending to Him for years. It was one of the things that led to my leaving Chicago a few years later to enter upon a worldwide ministry. If God had not in His infinite wisdom and love taken our beloved child, our beautiful and gifted child from us, I think I would never have seen China, Japan, Australia, New Zealand, India, and the marvelous work of God in these countries, and the great work of God that followed in England, Ireland, Wales, Germany, and many other places. God's judgments are *unsearchable . . . his ways past finding out!* (Romans 11:33), but they are always wise and loving, though we for the time cannot understand how. All of God's seemingly severe dealings with us came from the wise and wondrous love of God, and we both saw it and praised Him. There is no kinder manifestation of the love of God than His chastening when we forget Him or wander from Him or become immersed in the world.

One beautiful spring day years ago a friend of mine in Ohio asked me to take a drive with him. We drove out into the country to a quiet cemetery. We entered and went to a remote corner of the cemetery and found three graves side by side, one the grave of an adult and the other two of children. They were the graves of that man's wife and his two little girls, all the family he had at the time with the exception of one little boy. We knelt beside the graves in prayer. As we drove back to town that man said to me, "Brother Torrey, I pity the man whom God has not chastened."

What did he mean? He meant this: he had been a man of the world, an honorable, highly respected man, but a thoroughgoing worldling. Diphtheria came into his home. It took one of his little daughters. As she lay in her casket, the father knelt beside it and promised God that he would become a Christian. But when the first bitterness of the sorrow had passed, he forgot his vow. Again sickness and death entered his home. This time the second daughter died. Beside her coffin, he renewed his vow and kept it. He came to know the joy that every true Christian knows – to have the glorious hope for eternity that only the Christian has. I think he became the most active and efficient

Christian in the community, and it all came from God's chastening love. He told me again and again that his favorite text of Scripture was *whom the Lord loveth he chasteneth.* Ah, friends, if some affliction has come upon you, see it as a token of God's love and learn the sweet lessons He would teach by this sorrow.

God's Love Sympathizes with Us

God's love is also manifested in His sympathizing with us in all our afflictions. This is very clear in a wonderful verse in the Old Testament: *In all their affliction he was afflicted, and the angel of his presence saved them: in his love and in his pity he redeemed them; and he bare them, and carried them all the days of old* (Isaiah 63:9). While God, in His wise love for us, chastens us, even scourges us, when we forget Him and wander into sin and worldliness, nevertheless He deeply sympathizes with us in every sorrow, trial, and heartache that our sin brings upon us. *In all [our] affliction he [is] afflicted.*

It may be His own hand that sends the affliction, as it was in the passage just read; we need the affliction. It does us good, so He sends it; but He suffers with us in it. God is the one great sympathizer, for *in all [our] affliction he [is] afflicted.* In our own sorrow, we had many, many sympathizing human friends, and letters and telegrams of heartfelt sympathy poured in upon us. But no one sympathized with us so fully, so tenderly, so deeply, so intelligently as God Himself. He saw what no human eye could see and entered into it all.

There were many tender little ministries of His in those days of profound sorrow, and many wondrous, great ministries also. No human being will ever know what Mrs. Torrey and I passed through the night following the burial of our little child, and the next morning. The waters were deep. It seemed as if they would go over our heads, but One walked beside us.

It was God. He suffered with us. He kept His Word: *When thou passest through the waters, I will be with thee; and through the rivers, they shall not overflow thee: when thou walkest through the fire, thou shalt not be burned; neither shall the flame kindle upon thee* (Isaiah 43:2).

Some of you are in deep sorrow, some in sorrow of one kind and some in sorrow of an entirely different kind, but I want to tell you one and all that God sympathizes with you all in your sorrow whatever it may be. It may seem to you that no one sympathizes with you, that no one even understands, that no one cares, and that may be true of men, but it is not true of God. He understands it all and enters into it all. Our Father cares.

> God sympathizes with you all in your sorrow whatever it may be.

A woman came to see me at the hotel where I was staying in Bendigo, Australia. She told me that an awful sorrow had come into her life, but that she could not tell it to anyone, for they all knew her. But I was a stranger and would soon leave the place. Her burden was so heavy, she felt that she needed the sympathy of someone, so she had come to me. It was a terrible story that she told me. She was passing through one of the greatest sorrows that ever overtakes any true woman, and her heart was nearly crushed.

When she had finished that sad story, she said to me, "I feel better now that there is someone who knows my sorrow and can sympathize with me."

I said to her, "I do indeed sympathize with you. I am glad you came and told me the story that I might help you bear your burden. But," I added, "there is One who has known all about it from the beginning. God has known all about it and He has sympathized with you all the time." Oh, it is true; not a sorrow, not a heartache, not a disappointment, not a calamity, and not a grief ever comes to us without our heavenly Father knowing it all. He knows it in all its details and sympathizes with us in all the suffering; He Himself suffers far more than we suffer.

God's Love Always Remembers Us

God's love is manifested in His never forgetting those whom He loves. He Himself tells us in the wonderful words in Isaiah 49:15-16: *Can a woman forget her sucking child, that she should not have compassion on the son of her womb? yea, these may forget, yet will not I forget thee. Behold, I have graven thee upon the palms of my hands; thy walls are continually before me.*

God sometimes seems to forget, but He never does. We cry and no answer comes. The heavens seem to be as brass above our heads, but God has not forgotten. He never forgets. A mother may forget her child, and though that is not likely, she may forget. But God has said, *Yet will not I forget thee.* He has said furthermore, *Behold, I have graven thee upon the palms of my hands.*

God's Love Forgives

God's love is manifested in His forgiving our sins. Hezekiah cried unto the Lord, *Behold, it was for my peace that I had great bitterness: but thou hast in love to my soul delivered it from the pit of corruption; for thou hast cast all my sins behind thy back* (Isaiah 38:17). God stands ready in His love to pardon the sins of the vilest sinner. There are two things, and only two, which in His love He demands as a condition of that pardon. First, we must forsake our sins; second, we must turn to Him in faith and surrender to His will. Listen to His own Word: *Let the wicked forsake his way, and the unrighteous man his thoughts: and let him return unto the* Lord, *and he will have mercy upon him; and to our God, for he will abundantly pardon* (Isaiah 55:7).

God will not pardon our sins if we hold on to them. There is a theory regarding God's love current in the world today that has no warrant in the Word of God; namely, that because *God is love,* He will pardon and save all men whether they repent and believe on Jesus Christ or not.

This theory is wholly and utterly unscriptural. To believe it you must give up the Bible. But if you give up the Bible, you must give up your belief that *God is love,* for it is from the Bible and from the Bible alone that we learn that truth. There is absolutely no other proof that *God is love* than that the Bible says so. That is proof enough, for the Bible can be proven to be the Word of God. But if you give up the Bible and are logical, you must give up your belief that *God is love,* for when the Bible is gone, the belief that *God is love* has no foundation of any kind.

> God will not pardon our sins if we hold on to them.

But if you retain the Bible, you cannot believe that God will pardon and save all men whether they repent or not. The most illogical system in the world (except Unitarianism) is Universalism. It starts out with the Bible's statement that *God is love* as its foundation stone. Then it goes to work to discredit the Bible by rejecting other plain statements in it: statements about hell and the future state of those who reject Christ. By doing that, it undermines the authority of the Bible and thus undermines the foundation of our faith that *God is love.*

In other words, Universalism tries to build up a superstructure by undermining its own foundation. Give up the Bible and there is no proof that *God is love,* so Universalism is no longer possible. If you believe in the Bible, you must believe in hell, and so Universalism ceases. Take either horn of the dilemma you please, and Universalism has absolutely no foundation. The very love of God, God's love for the righteous and His love for His Son, Jesus Christ, demands that if men persist in sin and persist in the rejection of His Son, Jesus Christ, they must be separated from the righteous and punished. The love of God makes hell a necessity if men persist in sin. And if they persist eternally in sin, it makes eternal hell a necessity. It is psychologically certain, as well as clearly revealed in the Bible, that if men persist in sin beyond a certain point they will persist in sin eternally.

But if the vilest sinner repents, God will pardon. He says so. He goes so far as to say in Isaiah 1:18, *Come now, and let us reason together, saith the* Lord: *though your sins be as scarlet, they shall be as white as snow; though they be red like crimson, they shall be as wool.*

A man once said to me, "My sins are too great for God to pardon."

I answered, "I do not wish you to think that your sins are any less than you now think they are; no doubt they are even greater than you think; but I want you to see that great as your sins are, God's pardoning love is greater still."

How often God proved this in the Bible. David's sin was great, it was monstrous; he was an adulterer and a murderer, and yet God pardoned him. Manasseh's sin was exceedingly great; he hated God, and he hated God's people. He made the streets of Jerusalem to run with the blood of God's servants, and yet God pardoned him (2 Kings 24:3-4; cf. 2 Chronicles 33:1-13). Saul of Tarsus was a great sinner; he hated Jesus Christ. He persecuted the disciples of Jesus Christ and took part in their murder; he was a bold blasphemer and compelled others to blaspheme, and yet God pardoned him.

So down through the centuries many of the vilest sinners this world has ever seen have repented, and God has pardoned them. Many men and women have gone down into the deepest depths of sin, but God has pardoned and saved them, and they can rejoice in His pardoning love, knowing that their every sin is blotted out, and they have been transformed by the power of His grace.

God's Love Is Sacrificial

God's love was manifested in His giving His only begotten Son to die in our place. As the Spirit of God puts it in John 3:16: *For God so loved the world, that he gave his only begotten Son, that whosoever believeth in him should not perish, but have everlasting life.* And again we read in Romans 8:32: *He that spared not his own Son, but delivered him up for us all.* And we read in 1 John 4:10: *Herein is love, not that we loved God, but that he loved us, and sent his Son to be the propitiation for our sins.* And in the prophetic vision of the Old Testament, seven hundred years before the Savior was born, we read: *All we like sheep have gone astray; we have turned every one to his own way; and the* LORD *hath laid on him the iniquity of us all* (Isaiah 53:6). This manifestation of God's love is the greatest of all. This manifestation of God's love is stupendous; it seems past believing, but we know it is true. God made the greatest sacrifice in His power for our good. He made the greatest sacrifice in the world's history; He gave up that which was dearest to Him, HIS OWN SON.

No earthly son was ever so dear to his father as Jesus Christ was dear to God. I have a son, an only son, and I love him, but my love for my boy is but the faintest foreshadowing of God's love for Jesus Christ. And yet God gave that only begotten Son, that eternally beloved Son, up for you and me. He gave Him up to die, to die an awful death, an appalling death. He gave Him up to be crushed by the weight of man's sin and guilt. And for what purpose did He give Him up? *That whosoever believeth in him should not perish, but have everlasting life.* God has done everything in His power to provide everlasting life for each one of us. If we do not have it, it is our own fault. God has exhausted the resources of infinite wisdom and infinite love and infinite power to provide everlasting life for you and me, and you and I can have it for the taking.

Such is the love of God, very inadequately described. But I wish to ask a question in closing. The question is this: What are you going to do with that wondrous love of God right now?

Our guilt never looks so black as when seen in the dazzling light of God's amazing love. To be a sinful man or woman and to despise and break God's holy and excellent laws seems bad enough, but the worst thing, the most damnable and damning thing about men and women without Christ is that *they are trampling underfoot the love of God.* What would you think of a man who had a true and loving mother who had done everything for him, made every sacrifice for him, and had impoverished herself and imperiled and wasted her life for him, and then he despised that love, rejected that love, sneered at that love, denied that love, and sought to discredit that love? Would you not say that the man was a wretch? But no mother's love is so great and wonderful as the love of God for you and me. No mother ever made a sacrifice for her child as great as God has made for you and me. Now what will you do with that love? Will you accept it or despise it? Will you put your trust in it or spurn it? Will you open your heart to it or spit upon it? What will you do with it?

Are you rejecting Christ? Are you trampling underfoot the wondrous love of God revealed by giving His Son to die on Calvary's cross for you? If you are, what have you to say for yourselves? Give up your awful treatment of this glorious Son of God, and accept Him now as your personal Savior; surrender to Him as your Lord and Master and begin the confession of Him, a confession that many should have begun long, long ago. Go out to serve Him all the remainder of your days with all your strength.

Chapter 3

The Most Wonderful Sentence Ever Written

For God so loved the world, that he gave his only begotten Son, that whosoever believeth in him should not perish, but have everlasting life.
(John 3:16)

My text is the most wonderful sentence that was ever written. Of course, that sentence is in the Bible. All the greatest sentences that were ever written are found in one book, God's Word, the Bible. The Bible is a book that abounds in illuminating, stirring, startling, marvelous, bewildering, amazing, and life-transforming utterances – utterances with which there is absolutely nothing to compare in all the other literature of the world. But I am inclined to think that the one we are to consider here is the most remarkable of them all. I think that after we have given it careful thought, you will agree with me that this sentence is the most wonderful that was ever written.

You are most likely familiar with it. I doubt if there is a person in this audience who has not heard it again and again.

Indeed, our very familiarity with it has blinded many of us to its wonderful character and stupendous significance. But we are going to look at it steadily and closely, turning it around and around, as one would turn around and scrutinize a diamond of unusual purity, beauty, brilliance, and play of prismatic colors, until its beauty, its wisdom, its glory, its sublimity, and its amazing significance are more fully seen and appreciated by us.

The sentence is found in John 3:16: *For God so loved the world, that he gave his only begotten Son, that whosoever believeth in him should not perish, but have everlasting life.* There are whole volumes of incomparably precious truth packed into that one sentence. Indeed, many volumes have been devoted to the exposition of that one verse, but it is not exhausted yet and never will be. These marvelous words of God never become hackneyed, worn out, or wearisome. We are always beholding new beauty and new glory in them. When all the millions of volumes that men have written in many languages throughout the many centuries of literary history have become obsolete and forgotten, that imperishable sentence shall shine out in its matchless beauty and unequaled glory throughout the endless ages of eternity. Let me repeat it: *For God so loved the world, that he gave his only begotten Son, that whosoever believeth in him should not perish, but have everlasting life.* God Himself has used that statement to save thousands of souls, to lift men out of the sad, appalling ruin which sin had worked in the glory of likeness to Himself. I trust that He may use it now to save many more.

The verse tells us five exceedingly important facts: First, God's attitude toward the world; second, God's attitude toward sin; third, God's attitude toward His Son; fourth, God's attitude toward all who believe in His Son; fifth, God's attitude toward all who refuse or neglect to believe in His Son.

God's Attitude toward the World

First of all, this verse from God's Word tells us what God's attitude is toward the world. What is God's attitude toward the world? Love. The sentence reads: *God so loved the world, that he gave his only begotten Son, that whosoever believeth in him should not perish, but have everlasting life.* Love is the most wonderful thing in the world, and love is one of the most uncommon things in the world. Today there is much that is called love, but most of that which is called love is not love at all.

We often speak of a young man's love for a young woman, and all we mean is that this young man wishes to get that young woman for his own pleasure and gratification. That is not love at all; it often does not have the slightest resemblance of love. It is often utter selfishness and not infrequently the vilest and most unbridled lust. It is not unlikely that if the young woman refuses to accept him as a husband or so-called lover, he will shoot her down or seek to blast her reputation. And that hideous thing we call love! He "loved" her so much that he killed her. It is as remote from love as anything possibly can be, as remote from love as hell is from heaven. It is the lowest order of selfishness and the grossest beastliness.

A lawyer here in this city two weeks ago shot his former wife in the back, when she was not looking, because she would not return to him and endure more outrages that he had inflicted upon her for years. Was it love that prompted his amazingly cowardly, sneaking, cruel, ruffian, devilish act? No! It was a passion that would have disgraced the lowest wild beast of the jungle.

We speak of one man's love for another. What do we usually

mean? Only this – the two men are friendly because in many respects they are congenial and enjoy one another's company. But if one does some little thing that offends the other, the so-called love turns into utter indifference or even into bitter hate. It was never love. It was mere self-centered fondness.

All this is not love. What is love? Love is the consuming, absorbing desire for and delight in another's highest good. Real love is entirely unselfish. It utterly loses sight of self-interest and sets itself to seeking the interest of the person loved. This was God's attitude toward the world. He *loved* the world, really loved it.

He looked down upon this world, the whole mass of men living at any time and that would live in all times to come, and He loved them all. His whole being went out in infinite yearning to benefit and bless the world. Any cost to Himself would be disregarded if it would bless the world to pay the cost. *God so loved the world, that he gave his only begotten Son.* Oh, men and women, stand and wonder! Oh angels, archangel, cherubim, and seraphim, stand and wonder! *God so loved the world, that he gave his only begotten Son.*

Some men tell us that they cannot believe the Bible to be the Word of God because there are so many incredible statements in it. But John 3:16 is the most incredible statement in the whole Book, and yet we know it is true. If I can believe that statement, I shouldn't have any difficulty with any other statement in the whole Book; and I can believe that statement; I do believe that statement. I know that statement is true. I have put it to the test of personal experience and found it true. *God so loved the world, that he gave his only begotten Son* has been God's attitude toward the world from the beginning. That is God's attitude toward the world today.

God loves the world. There are men and women and children in this world whom you and I love, but God loves the whole world. There is not a man in it, not a woman in it, not a child in it whom God does not love. From the intellectually most gifted and morally most saintly man and woman down to the most morally, most degraded and brute-like man or woman in the slums of a great city or in the jungles of some cannibal island, God loves each and every one. *God so loved the world, that he gave his only begotten Son, that whosoever believeth in him should not perish, but have everlasting life.*

There are hundreds and hundreds of people who gather in this church, about whom you care absolutely nothing. You never saw them before; you will never see them again. If you should read in your paper tomorrow morning, "John Jones, who was at the Church of the Open Door, stepped in front of a Sixth Street car as he was going home from the service and was instantly killed," you would hardly give it a second thought. John Jones is nothing to you. But John Jones is something to God. God loves John Jones, and John Smith, and John Johnson, and every other man and woman and child.

> There is One who so loved you that He gave his only begotten Son to die for you, and that One is God.

You may be a lonely stranger in a great city's crowd. Perhaps you have been unfortunate and are penniless and friendless; perhaps you have gone down into some black depth of sin, and you say to yourself, "Not one person in this great crowd has the slightest interest in me," and that may be true. But there is One who has an interest in you. There is One who so loved you that He *gave his only begotten Son* to die for you, and that One is God. God loves the world and everyone in it. God loves the world in the purest, deepest, and highest sense of that word *love*. Yes, God loves you. "Whom do you mean by *you*?" someone asks. I mean every man, woman, and child.

There is nothing about the world to cause God to love it.

It is a sinful world; it is a selfish world; it is a corrupt world. The more I get to know the world of which I am a part, and the more I get to know myself, the more I am humbled. John was entirely right when he said, *The whole world lieth in the evil one* (1 John 5:19).

I am an optimist, but I am not an optimist by painting a black world white. Look at the rich world. What a cruel thing it is. How it marches on to greater wealth, trampling down everyone that lies in its path. How are great fortunes usually built up? You know. I know. By the trampling of human hearts under foot. But look at the poor world. It is nearly as cruel as the rich world.

One day in Chicago two men were working hard to make an honest living for themselves and their families just four doors north of the church where I was pastor. Four other poor men sneaked in and chopped their heads open with hatchets and ran.

Why did they do it? Simply because they wanted the jobs of these two men. The two men struck down by the four heartless cowards were guilty of no crime and no wrong against the ones that cut them down. They did not belong to the union; that was all. If you wish to know the spirit of the rich world, look at some of the greedy, conscienceless trusts. If you wish to know the spirit of the poor world, look at the present-day methods of the trade unions. The spirit of both is essentially the same: greed for gold. Money must be secured at any cost, even of the of murder of others by the slow process of starvation on the part of the rich, or the rapid process of hatchet and bullet and dynamite on the part of the poor.

A cruel, selfish, bloodthirsty world is this. What the world really is, we saw in the late war.[1] But God loves the world in such a way that He was willing to send His Son to die for us. God loves those four cowards who cut down their fellow laboring

---

[1] World War I

men enough to send His Son to die for them. God loves those millionaires who already have more than is needed for their own good or for the good of their families, but are trying to increase their wealth by crowding competitors out and pushing their families to the poorhouse, enough to send His Son to die for them. God loves those moral monsters that made Europe flow with blood and gasp with poison gas, enough to send His Son to die for them. As I come to know more and more of the cruelty, greed, selfishness, falsehood, wickedness, lust, vileness, and beastliness there is in this world, in the social world, high and low, in the business world in all its departments, and in the political world, I sometimes almost wonder why God does not blot out this whole world as He did Sodom and Gomorrah of old.

Why doesn't He do it? I will tell you why. God extends love to the world. In spite of all its cruelty, in spite of all its greed, in spite of all its selfishness, in spite of all its lust, in spite of all its vileness in thought and word and deed, God has love for the world. Isn't it wonderful, isn't it amazing that a holy God would extend love to a sinful world like this? But He does!

There is not a man whom God does not offer His love. There is not a woman whom God does not offer His love. There is not a thief whom God does not offer His love. There is not a woman who has forgotten her modesty and her true womanhood whom God does not offer His love. There is not an adulterer whom God does not offer His love, not a sinner, not an outcast, not a criminal of any kind whom God does not offer love. *God so loved the world, that he gave his only begotten Son, that whosoever believeth in him should not perish, but have everlasting life.*

Years ago I said to a woman who was in deep despair because of the depths of iniquity and infamy into which she had fallen, "God loves you."

"Not me, Mr. Torrey. God doesn't love me. I have killed a man," she cried.

"Yes, I know that, but God loves you."

"No, not me. I have murdered innocent, unborn babes."

"Yes, I know that, but God loves you."

"Not me. My heart is as hard as a rock."

"Yes, but God loves you."

"Not me. I have prayed to the devil to take away all my convictions, and he has done it."

"Yes, I know all that, but God loves you." Then I made that woman get down on her knees, and she came to believe in God's love for her, and she found a great peace.

I saw her again last month when I was in Chicago. At the close of one of my meetings, she came down to the platform to speak to me with others who crowded around me. She said, "Do you know me?"

I replied, "Of course I know you," and called her by name.

Her face was covered with smiles. "Oh," she said, "Mr. Torrey, I am still at the old work of winning others to Christ."

Ah, some self-righteous skeptics hold up their hands in holy horror and disgust, and say, "I don't want to believe in a God who welcomes sinners so vile as that." You miserable Pharisee, you old hypocrite, you are essentially as bad as she once was and infinitely worse than she now is. But God loves you, even you. God's attitude toward the whole wide world is love.

God's Attitude toward Sin

But what is God's attitude toward sin? Our text tells us that His attitude toward sin is hate. God loves the world with infinite love! God hates sin with infinite hate! How does our text show that? Listen. *God so loved the world, that he gave his only begotten Son, that whosoever believeth in him should not perish, but have everlasting life.*

How does that show that God hates sin? In this way: if God

had not hated sin, He could have saved the world that He loved without an atonement – without the atonement that cost Him so much, the death and agony of His only begotten Son, who died as an atoning sacrifice on the cross. But because God was holy and therefore hated sin, hated it with infinite hatred, His hatred of sin had to manifest itself either in the punishment of the sinner and the banishment of the sinner forever from Himself and from life and hope, or in some other way. But God's love would not permit the just punishment of the sinner. So God, in the person of His Son, took the penalty of sin upon Himself and thus saved the world He loved. *All we like sheep have gone astray; we have turned every one to his own way; and Jehovah hath made to strike on him the iniquity of us all* (Isaiah 53:6, exactly translated from the Hebrew). In this way God made possible eternal life for every sinner who would accept the salvation that He purchased for them by the atoning death of His only begotten Son.

> God made possible eternal life for every sinner who would accept the salvation that He purchased for them.

The cross of Christ declares two things: First, God's infinite love of the world; second, God's infinite hatred of sin. Oh, wicked man, do not assume that because God loves you, He will wink at your sin. Not for one moment. He hates your sin; He hates your greed; He hates your selfishness; He hates your cruelty; He hates your dishonesty; He hates your lying; He hates your drunkenness; He hates your impure imagination; He hates your moral uncleanness; He hates your beastliness; He hates every sin, great and small, of which you are guilty. The hatred of a true man for all falsehood, the hatred of honest men for all dishonesty, and the hatred of a true, pure woman for the unspeakable vileness of the woman of the street and gutter is nothing compared to the blazing wrath of God at your smallest sin.

God's Attitude toward His Son

This wonderful verse also tells of God's attitude toward His Son. What is God's attitude toward His Son? Listen. *God so loved the world, that he gave his only begotten Son.* God's attitude toward His Son, *his only begotten Son,* is infinite love. The Lord Jesus is the only Son of God. We become sons of God through our faith in Him, but He is the only Son of God by eternal and inherent right. He was the object of His Father's infinite love in the measureless ages before any one of the worlds was created; yes, before there was an angel or archangel or any of the heavenly beings.

Let me speak to you fathers. What is your attitude toward your son? How you love him. And if you have only one son, how intensely you love him. I have but one son. I have longed for more, but God in His wisdom has seen fit to give us but one son. How I love him! God only knows how I love him. But my love for my one son is nothing, nothing at all compared to God's love for His only begotten Son.

I sometimes think of my boy and think I know something of God's love for Jesus Christ, but it is only a little, a very little that I know. But though God thus loved His Son, God gave that Son, whom He so infinitely loved, that Son who through all eternity had been the object of His delight, God gave that only begotten Son for the world, for you and for me. He gave Him to leave heaven and His own companionship to come down to earth to live as a lonely stranger here. He gave Him to be spit upon, buffeted, and *despised and rejected of men.* He gave Him to be crowned with thorns, mocked, and derided. He gave Him to be dragged through the streets before a howling, yelling, jeering mob. He gave Him to be nailed to the cross. Yes, to a cross! And to hang there in misery, pain, and agony for hours, the object of the rude jests and jeers of the merciless mob. He gave Him to die of a broken heart, a heart broken by the reproach of the men He loved (Psalm 69:20), and by grief over man's sins which He had taken upon Himself. Yes, God gave Him, *his only begotten Son,* thus to be separated from Himself, to suffer, and to die. Why? Because God loved you and me, and that was the only price that would purchase our salvation. And God paid that price, that awful price.

Oh, it is wonderful! I can think of but one other thing that is anywhere near as astonishing as the love of God for sinners. What is that? The way we treat that love. The way men treat it. The way some of you despise it. The way you reject it. The way you trample it under foot. The way you even try to doubt it, disbelieve it, deny it, discredit it, and try to make yourself think that you have "intellectual difficulties about the doctrine of the atonement."

At least be honest. Your real difficulty is not intellectual; you want to save your pride and excuse the enormity of your ingratitude. And to do that you do not hesitate at the gross sin of even denying the Lord that bought you, bought you by His atoning agony and death (2 Peter 2:1). Oh, be honest with the wondrous love of God, even if you are determined to spurn it. Your pretended "theological difficulties with the atonement" that Jesus Christ made upon the cross are simply your dishonest attempts to excuse your abominable ingratitude and damnable rejection of infinite love. Bear with me for talking so plainly about your sin. I do it in love for you. You may not be willing to admit that today, but you will have to admit it in that day when you stand in the light of the great white throne where all lies and pretexts and deceptions and hypocrisies will be burned up.

God's Attitude toward Believers in Christ

Let us look at another thing: what our sentence teaches about God's attitude toward believers in the Lord Jesus Christ. What is God's attitude toward all who believe in Jesus Christ? It can be put in a few words. God's attitude toward all believers in Jesus Christ is to give them eternal life. *God so loved the world, that he gave his only begotten Son, that whosoever believeth in him should not perish, but have everlasting life.*

The death of Jesus Christ has opened for all who believe in Him a way of pardon, and made it possible for a holy God to forgive sin and to give eternal life to the vilest sinner if only he will believe on Jesus Christ. *The wages of sin is death,* and these wages must be paid; but Jesus Christ paid the price, so life and not death is possible for you and me; *the free gift of God is eternal life in Christ Jesus our Lord* (Romans 6:23). *Whosoever* believes on Jesus Christ, whom God gave to die for him, can have eternal life; yes, he does have eternal life.

> He is infinitely worthy of your faith.

Anyone can have eternal life. There is but one condition – just believe on Jesus Christ. You ought to do it anyhow, even if there were nothing to be gained by your believing on Him; you owe it to Jesus Christ to believe on Him. He is infinitely worthy of your faith.

But there *is* something to be gained by believing on Him, something of infinite worth – eternal life. Do you desire eternal life? You can have it. Anyone can have it, no matter what his past may have been. *God so loved the world, that he gave his only begotten Son, that whosoever believeth in him should not perish, but have everlasting life.* Oh, if I offered you great honor, it would be nothing compared with this. If I offered you enormous wealth, it would be nothing compared with this. If I offered you exemption from all sickness and pain, it would be nothing compared with this. Eternal life! That is what God offers. And God offers it to each one of you. Oh, how it makes the heart swell and throb with hope and joy and rapture – eternal life!

God's Attitude toward Those Who Will Not Believe in Jesus Christ

There is just one thing left to mention, and that is God's attitude toward all those who will not believe on Jesus Christ. What is it? Listen. *For God so loved the world, that he gave his only begotten Son, that whosoever believeth on him should not perish, but have everlasting life.* God's attitude toward those who will not believe on Jesus Christ, those who prefer sin and vanity and pride to the glorious Son of God, is simply this: God with great grief and reluctance withdraws from them the infinite gift He has purchased at so great a cost and which they will not accept. God leaves them to perish. There is no hope for any man who rejects God's gift of eternal life, obtained by simply believing in His only begotten Son. God has exhausted all the possibilities of a saving love and power in Jesus Christ's atonement on the cross of Calvary. Reject Him, neglect to accept Him, and you must eternally perish.

God's attitude toward the world is infinite love. God's attitude toward sin is infinite hatred. God's attitude toward His Son is unutterable love, but He gave that Son up to die for you and me. God's attitude toward the believer is to give him eternal life, regardless of what his past has been. God's attitude toward those who will not believe is to leave them to the hell they so madly choose. Men and women, what will you choose today: life or death? Some of you will decide that question in a few minutes; decide it for all eternity. God help you to decide it right.

One night years ago in Minneapolis, I knelt in prayer beside a young woman who was having an awful struggle. A fearful battle was going on in her soul between the forces of light and the forces of darkness. She heard God calling her to accept His love and to accept the eternal life that His love had purchased by the atoning death of His own Son. But she heard other voices too, voices of the world and the voice of Satan himself, luring her to turn her back on Jesus Christ and choose the world. It was awful to watch the battle, and my heart ached as I watched, and I kept crying to God that the Holy Spirit might gain the victory. Now and then I spoke to her.

Finally, I took out my watch and said, "This battle cannot last much longer. Continue to resist the Holy Spirit as you are resisting Him now, and you will seal your doom. I believe if you do not yield to God in the next ten minutes, you will never yield but will be lost forever." Then I prayed but said nothing more to her, but now and again looked at my watch. The fight went on. Which way would she decide? Before the ten minutes were up, she yielded to God.

There is a similar battle going on in the hearts of some who are reading these words. Some of you have been brought to realize the wondrous love of God for you as you have never realized it before. Some of you have been brought to see that eternal life is possible for you today if you will only choose Christ. But the power of the world and of sin and of Satan is strong upon you; the world, sin, and above all – Satan – will not let you go without making a mighty effort to keep you in his power, to blind you and forever destroy your soul.

Men and women who do not know Christ, each and every one of you, look, look, look! Look once more at the cross of Christ. See Him hanging there in awful agony, paying the penalty for your sin; and as you look, listen once more to the precious words of the most wonderful sentence that was ever written: *God so loved the world, that he gave his only begotten Son, that whosoever believeth in him should not perish, but have everlasting life.* What will you do with that love today? Will you yield to it, believe in the Savior, and obtain eternal life? Or will you trample that wondrous love of God under foot and say again, as you have often said, "I will not accept Christ," and go out to perish, perish eternally?

One night, many years ago, I was preaching the first sermon I ever preached in the city of Chicago. (It was some years before I went there to live.) I was at the first International Convention of Christian Workers. The morning the convention opened, I entered a little late, and the nominating committee was just bringing in its report. And to my amazement, I heard them announce my name as nominated for chairman of the convention and president of the International Christian Workers' Association. I was not yet thirty years old, and there were many workers there who knew far more about aggressive methods of Christian work than I had ever learned.

However, there was nothing to do but to accept the position, and during the days of that wonderful convention, I occupied the chairman's seat. The convention was held in the old First Methodist Church in the heart of the city at the corner of Washington and Clark Streets. When Sunday came, of course, the church held its own services, but I was invited to preach at the evening service. There had been much prayer, and the Spirit of God was present in great power. When I gave out the invitation, many rose to say that they would accept Jesus Christ as their Savior and then came down to the altar. Among those who had risen, I noticed a beautifully dressed lady near the front, an intelligent-looking woman; but I noticed also that she did not come to the altar with the others. While the altar service was in progress, I stepped down and urged her to come to the front, but she refused.

On Monday night, at the regular session of the convention, I saw her come in and take a seat just a few rows from the back of the building. When the meeting was drawing to a close, I called Mayor Howland of Toronto (who was vice president of the convention) to the chair and slipped down to the back of the church in order to speak with this lady before she got out of the building. The moment the benediction was pronounced,

I hurried to her side and asked if she would remain for a few moments. As the others passed by, she sat down, and I took a seat beside her and urged her to an immediate and wholehearted acceptance of Jesus Christ.

"Let me tell you my story," she replied. "I have attended a Sunday school in this city ever since I was a little girl. I scarcely missed a Sunday." (She told me which Sunday school it was; one of the aristocratic Sunday schools on the North Side.) "But," she continued, "though I have been going to Sunday school all these years, do you know that you are the first person in all my life that ever spoke to me personally about my accepting Christ?"

Then she went on to tell me the story of her life. She was unusually well educated, occupying a high position of responsibility, but the story that she told me of her career was so shameless that I was amazed that a woman of sense, to say nothing of character, would dream of telling such a story to a man. Then she hurried on and told me how she had spent the preceding Easter Sunday. It was a story I could not repeat. Having finished, she said with a mocking laugh, "Funny way to spend Easter, wasn't it?"

I was astounded and shocked. I did not attempt to say anything in reply; I did not wish to. I simply opened my Bible to John 3:16, handed it to her and asked her to read it. It was a small Bible, and she had to hold it close to her face to see the words. She began to read with a smile on her lips: *For God so loved the world* (the smile vanished; she read on), *that he gave his only begotten Son*. She choked and broke down; the tears literally poured from her eyes on the page of the Bible and on the beautiful silk robe she wore. The love of God had conquered that sinful, hardened, trifling, seemingly shameless heart. Oh friend, I wish that His love might break your heart, break down your hardness, unbelief, worldliness, and resistance to God and His love. See the Lord Jesus hanging on yonder cross in unutterable agony and in indescribable pain, His heart breaking for you, breaking for your sins. Hear again this most wonderful sentence that was ever written: *For God so loved the world, that he gave his only begotten Son, that whosoever believeth in him should not perish, but have everlasting life.*

Chapter 4

The Only Gospel That Has Saving Power

For I am not ashamed of the gospel: for it is the power of God unto salvation to every one that believeth; to the Jew first, and also to the Greek. (Romans 1:16)

But though we, or an angel from heaven, should preach unto you any gospel other than that which we preached unto you, let him be anathema. As we have said before, so say I now again, if any man preacheth unto you any gospel other than that which ye received, let him be anathema. (Galatians 1:8-9)

My subject is "The Only Gospel That Has Saving Power." I have two texts: Romans 1:16 and Galatians 1:8-9.

We hear much in these days about various gospels. Some extol the gospel of social service; others talk of the gospel of the universal fatherhood of God and the universal brotherhood of man; and others speak of the gospel of work, the social gospel, or various other gospels. But there is but one real gospel, only one gospel that in actual fact has saving power. That gospel is *the gospel of Christ,* the gospel which Paul preached and of which he said that if any man, or even an angel from heaven, should preach any other gospel, he would be accursed of God.

All these gospels have one fatal fault: They don't save. These other gospels may sound virtuous; they may be described with enchanting rhetoric; they may be preached with great eloquence, with marvelous beauty of diction, with charming figures of speech; they may seem exceedingly alluring, but they don't save. For all their pretenses and prettiness, instead of saving, they darken, debase, and damn. They do not enlighten, elevate, and save.

Man's Need of Salvation

What man needs is salvation, not mere social uplift, moral improvement, or intellectual enlightenment. Man is lost. Every man is lost until he is definitely saved. The only thing that will save him is the gospel that Paul preached.

Every man needs salvation from the guilt of sin. Every man and woman on this earth is a sinner. Every man and woman on this earth has been a great sinner. Every man and woman on this earth has broken the first and greatest of God's commandments, namely, *Thou shalt love the Lord thy God with all thy heart, and with all thy soul, and with all thy mind* (Matthew 22:37-38).

> Every one of us is a guilty sinner in the sight of a holy God, and we need salvation from the guilt of sin.

Every one of us, therefore, is a guilty sinner in the sight of a holy God, and we need salvation from the guilt of sin. That is the first need, the great need, the crying need, the fundamental need of every one of us.

But every man also needs salvation from the power of sin.

Sin has a hold upon every one of us, a mastery over every one of us *that we cannot overcome in our own strength. We must find a deliverer from the power of sin.* The one universal need is the need of salvation, the need of salvation from the guilt and power of sin.

The gospel has power to save. As our text puts it, *the gospel is the power of God unto salvation to every one that believeth; to the Jew first, and also to the Greek,* and no other religion or philosophy has power to save; nothing else in all the world has power to save from the guilt and power of sin.

What Is the Gospel?

We come now right to the question, What is the gospel that has power to save? *Gospel* means, as I presume you all know, "good news" or "glad tidings." What is the good news, or the glad tidings, that has saving power in it? Paul himself tells us what this gospel was that he preached and of which he said, *It is the power of God unto salvation to every one that believeth.* We are not left to speculate about that, for Paul himself defines in the simplest and most easily understood terms exactly what the gospel was that he preached, the gospel that had saving power, and the only gospel that has saving power. Paul's full, and at the same time very plain, description of the gospel which he preached is in 1 Corinthians 15:1-4: *Now I make known unto you brethren, the gospel which I preached unto you, which also ye received, wherein also ye stand, by which also ye are saved; I make known, I say, in what words I preached it unto you, if ye hold it fast, except ye believed in vain.* And now comes the description of the gospel: *For I delivered unto you first of all that which also I received, how that Christ died for our sins according to the scriptures; and that he was buried; and that he hath been raised on the third day according to the scriptures.*

Notice first of all, in regard to this gospel that Paul preached, that the good news is *facts,* not theories, not speculations, not guesses, but solid, substantial, established, unmistakable, inescapable, absolutely sure facts. I am glad of that. Most of the gospels one hears today are mere theories. The gospel of Christ is facts, and the facts that constitute the good news were three.

First, *Christ died for our sins.* That certainly is good news. You and I are sinners. Every one of us has sinned. If anyone today seeks to deny that he is a sinner, his denial that he is a sinner does not make him any less a sinner; indeed, it makes him even more a sinner, for it makes him a liar as well as a sinner in other respects. As we read in 1 John 1: 8, 10: *If we say that we have no sin, we deceive ourselves, and the truth is not in us. If we say that we have not sinned, we make [God] a liar, and his word is not in us.*

So, by the denial of our sin, we do not make ourselves any less sinners, but we prove ourselves to be liars and make ourselves guilty of the enormous sin of making God a liar. That is what every Christian Scientist does; he makes God a liar, and that is what everyone else who denies that he is a sinner does; he makes God a liar. God says that we are sinners, and when we deny that fact, we give the lie to God. Every man, therefore, who denies that he is a great sinner is a liar, and all liars, unless they repent, are bound for the eternal fire, for God says in Revelation 21:8, *The fearful, and unbelieving, and abominable, and murderers, and fornicators, and sorcerers, and idolaters, and all liars, their part shall be in the lake that burneth with fire and brimstone; which is the second death.*

> By the denial of our sin we prove ourselves to be liars and make ourselves guilty of the enormous sin of making God a liar.

But not only are we sinners, but God is also holy, infinitely holy, and cannot tolerate sin. God is *of purer eyes than to behold evil,* and He *canst not look on iniquity,* and some day you and I must meet Him (Habakkuk 1:13). We must meet Him bearing our sin, carrying all our own sin upon us, or find someone else to bear our sin for us. If we should meet this Holy God with our sin upon us, then we must be forever banished from His presence and *be punished with everlasting destruction from the presence of the Lord, and from the glory of his power* (2 Thessalonians 1:9).

But the gospel tells us that someone else has borne our sin in our place. It tells us that a competent sin-bearer has been found. It tells us that *Christ died for our sins,* that the Lord Jesus paid our debt, all the debt we owe, that though "sin had left a crimson stain, He washed it white as snow."[2] Even Isaiah, seven hundred years before Christ, got a glimpse of this wonderful truth of the gospel. Speaking in the Holy Spirit, he said, *All we like sheep have gone astray; we have turned every one to his own way; and the* LORD *hath laid on him the iniquity of us all* (Isaiah 53:6).

So if we accept the Lord Jesus who died for our sins as our substitute Savior, then no matter how long we have sinned, no matter how greatly we have sinned, we can meet God with absolutely no sin upon us, for God Himself has put it upon another. So the Lord Jesus, by His death, saves us completely from all the guilt of sin.

The second fact that goes to make up the gospel is that *the Lord Jesus was buried.* At first sight, it is not clear how this is "good news," but it is good news; the fact of His burial shows the reality of His death and the actuality and literalness of His resurrection. The burial of Jesus Christ shows that the death of Jesus Christ was no sham death, no mere illusion; it was not merely a mortal thought, as the Christian Scientists would have us believe. It was a real death, and therefore it was a real

---

2   Elvina M. Hall, "Jesus Paid It All," 1865.

atonement. All that Christian Science and various other false systems offer us is a sham atonement for imaginary sin, and thus they offer us only a sham salvation. The gospel of Christ, the gospel that God makes known, the gospel that Paul preached, the gospel of a Savior who not only died but was also buried offers us a real atonement for sins that we know are very real and very great, and therefore it offers us a real salvation from the guilt of sin. This true gospel says to the vilest sinner in the world, "There is perfect pardon and justification for you, for the Son of God really died; He was really buried; and there is therefore a real and perfect salvation for you from all your guilt. *The blood of Jesus Christ his Son cleanseth us from all sin*" (1 John 1:7).

The third fact in the good news is that *Jesus Christ rose again,* or as Paul puts it in his description of the gospel in 1 Corinthians 15:4: *He hath been raised on the third day according to the scriptures.* That is certainly good news; it is great news. It is good news for many reasons, but especially good news from the standpoint of salvation, because it shows that Jesus Christ cannot only save all from the guilt of sin by His atoning death, but that He can also save all from the power of sin by His resurrection power. As it is put in that wonderful verse in Hebrews: *Wherefore also he is able to save to the uttermost them that draw near unto God through him, seeing he ever liveth to make intercession for them* (Hebrews 7:25). We need not only salvation from the guilt of sin, but we also need just as much salvation from the power of sin.

Suppose I were a great sinner and through faith in Christ crucified should find salvation from all my guilt, and perfect peace of conscience, and go out of here today very happy in the thought that all my sins were blotted out. Then suppose that tomorrow the same old temptations that have overcome me in the past, for example, the appetite for drink, some form of lust or impurity, an appetite for drugs, or an ungovernable temper, should confront me, and I had no power to resist the temptation, and down I go – how much would such a salvation be worth? But Jesus Christ not only died and was buried, He also rose again. Today He lives and has all power in heaven and on earth, so He can save me from my appetite for drink, the power of any evil desire, my temper, or whatever my sin may be; however weak I may be, I can begin here and now to live a clean and victorious life.

The following incident of a man who once called upon me in Chicago I have related before. This man sought a private interview, and when we had taken our seats alone in Mr. Moody's office, the man said, "I want to tell you my story." He went on as follows: "I am a Scotchman. When I was a child of seven over in Scotland, I began to read the Bible through. One day I came to a passage in Deuteronomy that told me that if I should keep the law of God a hundred years and then break it at one point after having kept it a hundred years, I would be under the curse of the broken law of God. Was that right?"

> But Jesus Christ not only died and was buried, He also rose again. Today He lives and has all power in heaven and on earth.

"Yes," I replied, "the Bible doesn't put it in just that way, but the Bible does say, *Cursed be he that confirmeth not the words of this law to do them*" (Deuteronomy 27:26).

"That's the passage," he said, "that I found, and I knew that I had already broken the law of God, and therefore I knew that I was under the curse of the broken law. Though I was only seven years of age, I was in deep distress. Night after night, I went to bed and wept myself to sleep, thinking how I was under the curse of the broken law of God. But I went on reading my Bible, and the next year when I was eight years old, I came to John 3:16. *For God so loved the world, that he gave his only begotten Son, that whosoever believeth in him should not perish, but have everlasting life.* And all my burden rolled away. Was I converted?"

"Well," I replied, "that sounds like a good, evangelical conversion."

"Let me tell you the rest of my story," he continued. "I grew up to manhood. I came to America; I came out here to Chicago and found work down in the stockyards. I am living down in the stockyards. Now, the stockyards, as you know, are a hard place, and I got to drinking, and every little while I go off on a drunk. What I have come to ask you is if there is any way in which I can get victory over the drink."

"You have come just to the right place," I replied. "I can answer your question. There *is* a way in which you can get victory over the drink. You have only believed half the gospel, and therefore you have only got half a salvation." I said, "Let me show you the whole gospel," and I opened to the fifteenth chapter of 1 Corinthians and read, *"Moreover, brethren, I declare unto you the gospel which I preached unto you, which also ye have received, and wherein ye stand; by which also ye are saved, if ye keep in memory what I preached unto you, unless ye have believed in vain. For I delivered unto you first of all that which I also received, how that Christ died for our sins according to the scriptures; and that he was buried, and that he rose again the third day according to the scriptures"* (1 Corinthians 15:1-4).

"Now," I went on, "you have believed the first part of this gospel, that Christ died and was buried, and through believing that, you have found pardon and peace."

"Yes."

"But," I continued, "that is only half the gospel. There is another half to it, and that is *that he rose again.* Do you believe that?"

"I believe everything in the Bible," he replied.

Again I asked, "Do you believe that Jesus rose again the third day?"

"Yes, I do."

"Very well, then. If He rose the third day, then He has all power in heaven and on earth."

"Yes."

"And He has power to keep you from the power of the drink and from the power of sin. Do you believe that?"

"Yes," he said, "I do."

"Will you trust Him to do it?"

"I will," he replied.

"Let us kneel down and tell God so," I said.

We knelt side by side. I prayed first and then he prayed. These were about the words he uttered: "Oh God, I have been believing half the gospel, and I have had half a salvation. I have believed that part of the gospel that told me that Christ died for my sins according to the Scriptures, and through believing that, I have found pardon and peace. But now I have come to believe the other half of the gospel, that Christ not only died but that He also rose again, that He has all power in heaven and on earth, and that He has power to keep me from the power of the drink."

Then he changed his mode of address and commenced speaking directly to Jesus Christ. "Lord Jesus," he said, "I believe that You are risen from the dead, and I believe that You have all power in heaven and on earth. I believe that You have power to save me from the drink. Oh Lord Jesus, save me from the power of drink right now. I ask it in Your name. Amen."

As he still knelt there with his head bowed in prayer, I said, "Did you really trust Him to do it?"

He replied, "I did." He rose, and I gave him some instruction as to how to make a success of this life upon which he had entered. He left the office, and I didn't hear from him for some weeks. Then I received a brief letter, but the letter was very much to the point. It said, "Dear Mr. Torrey, I am so glad I came to see you. *It works.*"

Yes, thank God, it does work. It works with anyone who really believes it. The gospel of a Savior who died and was buried and rose again has power to save from the guilt of sin, and it also has power to save from the power of sin. It has power *to save to the uttermost* those who come to God through Jesus Christ. And it is the only gospel that can do it. The gospel of Christian Science with a sham death and a sham resurrection cannot do it. The gospel of New Thought cannot do it. The gospel of theosophy cannot do it. The gospel of social service, of which we hear so much today, cannot do it. No gospel but the gospel of Jesus Christ, the gospel of a Savior who really died, who was really buried, and who really rose again can do it.

A short while ago a well-known pastor in Los Angeles announced that he was going to preach a gospel "without an atonement of blood." Well, if he does, he will preach a gospel that cannot save; he will preach a gospel that will send men to hell and not a gospel that will ever fit men for heaven. And anyone who preaches a gospel that Christ died but not a gospel that He rose again will preach a gospel that will not save from the power of sin. But the gospel contained in this blessed Book of God, the gospel that Jesus both died and rose again, will save. It will save from both the guilt and the power of sin; it will *save to the uttermost.*

Whom the Gospel Saves

But whom does the gospel save? It does not save everybody. This gospel has been proclaimed for more than eighteen hundred years, but it has not saved everybody yet, and it never will. There are many in these days who say the gospel is a failure because the great majority of men and women are not saved. They say, "Christianity is a failure, because after eighteen centuries our governments are not Christian, and wars and other damnable things are still possible."

But herein lies their mistake: God never intended the gospel to save everybody. He never gave it to save everybody. He never expected it to save everybody. He gave it to save those who would believe it and only those. It is not Christianity that has failed but man that has failed by rejecting this glorious gospel. The gospel has not failed because it has not saved everybody any more than a perfectly good medicine that will cure anybody who takes it fails when it doesn't cure those who don't take it. God has told us plainly from the beginning just who the gospel would save. Who does it save? Listen. *The gospel . . . is the power of God unto salvation to every one that believeth.* This tells us whom the gospel saves.

> It is not Christianity that has failed but man that has failed by rejecting this glorious gospel.

First, *it saves those who believe.* Not those who hear, but those who believe. The gospel does not save everyone who hears it. Millions of men have heard the gospel all through their lives, but died in their sins and went to hell. There are many who think that merely hearing the gospel or living in a Christian land makes them Christians.

One night I approached a very intelligent-looking man in Duluth, Minnesota. I said to him, "Are you a Christian?"

He replied, "Certainly; do you think I am a Muslim?" He thought that simply because he was born and brought up in a Christian land and heard the gospel, he was a Christian, but that does not make him a Christian. *Believing* the gospel, not merely hearing it, is what saves. Believing the gospel and not merely hearing it is what makes one a Christian. The gospel does not even save the one who merely admires it. A man may have a great admiration for the gospel, for the profound philosophy of the Bible, and yet be an utterly unsaved man. The gospel saves the one who believes it, and him alone. The one who believes what? The gospel. Really believes it, believes it with the heart. The one who has that kind of faith is led to action.

That faith will lead you to accept Christ as your atoning Savior and trust God to forgive you simply because Jesus Christ died in your place. It will lead you to accept Christ as your risen Savior and trust Him to deliver you from the power of sin. Having accepted Him, this faith will lead you to present an open confession of Him before the world. For it is written: *If thou shalt confess with thy mouth Jesus as Lord, and shalt believe in thy heart that God raised him from the dead, thou shalt be saved: for with the heart man believeth unto righteousness; and with the mouth confession is made unto salvation* (Romans 10:9-10).

This faith saves *every one that believeth.* As it says in our text, the gospel *is the power of God unto salvation to every one that believeth.* There is not a man or woman today whom the gospel cannot save. There is not a man or woman in the world so sunken in sin, so lost to all that is good and true and pure, that the gospel cannot save, if they will only believe. There is not a man or woman so utterly weak and helpless in sin that the gospel will not save them, if they believe it.

Why, then, is there a man or woman in the world who is not saved? Why is there a man or woman in the world who is not saved from the guilt and power of sin? Simply because he or she will not believe.

Let me illustrate. There is a great Mogul engine on the track. It is coaled and has water in the boiler; there is fire under the boiler; the steam is up, and there is a full head of steam. There is power in that locomotive to draw a heavily loaded freight train up the steepest grade; then that locomotive backs down to the train. The engineer reverses the lever, and the locomotive starts

THE ONLY GOSPEL THAT HAS SAVING POWER

up the grade, but not a car moves. Why not? Was it because there was no power in the locomotive to draw the train? No, there was plenty of power for that. What was the trouble? The brakeman had not put the coupling pin in.

Then the locomotive backs down again and backs up to the train of cars. The brakeman goes between the tender of the locomotive and the train; he drops in a little coupling pin. Then the engineer reverses the lever, and the locomotive starts up the track again. This time the train moves up the grade.

In the same way the gospel has power to save, if you *couple on*. The gospel locomotive stands on the track; there is power in that locomotive to carry the train most heavily loaded with sin up the track; steam is up, and it is starting up the grade to glory. It can pull you, no matter how heavily weighted you are with tons of sin, up the grade to glory. Fall in line. Couple on. Faith is the coupling pin. Just believe the gospel. It is up to every man and woman to say whether they will be saved or not, saved right now from the guilt and power of sin. It all depends upon whether they will or will not believe the gospel. Will you believe? *For I am not ashamed of the gospel: for it is the power of God unto salvation to every one that believeth.*

> It is up to every man and woman to say whether they will be saved or not.

Chapter 5

The Great Attraction: The Uplifted Christ

And I, if I be lifted up from the earth, will draw all men unto myself. (John 12:32)

A recent advertisement of a Sunday evening service in one of our American cities stated that there would be three attractions: a high-class movie, a popular gospel pianist and his wife, and a song from the opera *Madam Butterfly,* rendered by a well-known prima donna. It is startling when an unusually gifted and popular preacher, or his advertising committee, thinks the gospel of the Son of God has lost its power to draw, so it must be bolstered by adding a selection from a questionable opera, rendered by a professional opera singer, to help our once-crucified and now-glorified Savior and Lord.

This advertisement set me to thinking: What really was the great attraction to men today as well as in former days? At once, there came to my mind the words of our text containing God's answer to this question: *And I, if I be lifted up from the earth, will draw all men unto myself.* Nothing draws like the uplifted Christ. Movies may get a crowd of empty-headed and empty-hearted young men, women, and even middle-aged folks without brains or moral earnestness for a time, but nothing really draws and holds the men and women who are worthwhile like Jesus Christ lifted up. Nineteen centuries of Christian history prove the drawing power of Jesus when He is properly presented to men. I have seen some wonderful verifications of the assertion of our text as to the marvelous drawing power of the uplifted Christ.

In London, for two continuous months, six afternoons and evenings each week, I saw the great Royal Albert Hall filled and even jammed, and sometimes as many turned away as got in, though it would seat ten thousand people by actual count and stand two thousand more in the dome. On the opening night of these meetings, a leading reporter of the city of London came to me before the service began and said, "You have taken this building for two consecutive months?"

"Yes."

"And you expect to fill it every day?"

"Yes."

"Why," he said, "no one has ever attempted to hold two weeks' consecutive meetings here of any kind. Gladstone[3] himself could not fill it for two weeks. And you really expect to fill it for two months?"

I replied, "Come and see." He came and he saw.

On the last night, when the place was jammed to its utmost capacity, and thousands outside clamored for admission, he came to me again, and I said, "Has it been filled?"

He smiled and said, "It has." But what filled it? No show on earth could have filled it once a day for many consecutive days. The preacher was no remarkable orator. He had no gift

---

[3] William Ewart Gladstone was a British statesman and liberal politician. He had a career that lasted over sixty years with twelve years as prime minister of the United Kingdom and twelve years as chancellor of the Exchequer. He was affectionately known as "The People's William."

of wit and humor; he would not have exercised it if he had. The newspapers constantly called attention to the fact that he was no orator, but the crowds came and came and came; rainy days and sunny days, they crowded in or stood outside, often in a downpour of rain, in the vain hope of getting in. What drew them? The uplifted Christ, preached and sung in the power of the Holy Spirit, given in answer to the daily prayers of forty thousand people scattered throughout the earth.

In Liverpool, Tournament Hall sat around 12,500 comfortably. It was located in a very out-of-the-way part of the city, several blocks from the nearest streetcar line, perhaps half a mile from all the regular streetcar lines. That hall was filled night after night for three months, and on the last night they crowded 15,000 people into the building at seven o'clock, then emptied it, and crowded another 15,000 in who had been patiently waiting outside. Thirty thousand people were drawn in a single night! By what? By whom? Not by the preacher, not by the singer, but by Him who had said nearly nineteen hundred years before, *And I, if I be lifted up from the earth, will draw all men unto myself.*

The Exact Meaning of the Text

First, notice who the speaker is and what the circumstances were under which He spoke. The speaker was our Lord Jesus. Not the Christ of men's imaginings, but the Christ of reality, the Christ of actual historical fact. Not the Christ of Mary Baker Eddy's silly fantasy or of Madam Besant's mystical imaginings, but the Christ of actuality. The Christ who lived here among men and was seen, heard, and touched by men and who was soon to die a real death to save real sinners from a real hell to a real heaven is the speaker.

These were the circumstances: certain Greeks among those

who had come to worship at the Jewish feast came to the apostle Philip and said, *We would see Jesus.* Philip went to Andrew and told Andrew what these Greeks said. Andrew and Philip together came and told Jesus. In the heart-cry of these Greeks, *We would see Jesus,* our Lord recognized the yearning of the universal heart, the heart of the Greek as well as the Jew, for a satisfying Savior. The Greeks had their philosophers and sages, their would-be satisfiers and saviors, the greatest the world has ever known – Socrates, Aristotle, Plato, Epictetus, Epimenides, and many others. But they did not save, and they did not satisfy, and the Greeks cried, *We would see Jesus.* In their eagerness, Jesus foresaw the millions of all nations who would flock to Him when He had been crucified as the universal Savior, meeting all the needs of all mankind, so He cried, *And I, if I be lifted up from the earth, will draw all men unto myself.*

In the second place, notice the words *if I be lifted up.* To what does Jesus refer? The next verse answers the question. *But this he said, signifying by what manner of death he should die* (John 12:33). Jesus referred to His lifting-up on the cross to die as an atoning Savior for all mankind. This verse is often quoted as if it meant that if we lifted up Christ in our preaching, He would draw men. That is true, and it is a crying shame that we do not hold just Him up more in our preaching, and we would draw far more people if we did. But that is not our Lord's meaning. The lifting-up clearly referred to His being lifted up by His enemies on the cross to expose Him to awful shame and to an agonizing death, not to His not being lifted up in our preaching. It is the crucified Christ who draws; it is the crucified Christ who meets the deepest needs of the hearts of all mankind. It is an atoning Savior, a Savior who atones for the sins of men by His death and thus saves them from the holy wrath of an infinitely holy God, who meets the needs of men and thus draws all men, for all men are sinners. Preach any Christ but a crucified Christ, and you will not draw men for long. Preach any gospel but a gospel of atoning blood, and it will not draw for long.

Unitarianism does not draw men. Unitarian churches are born only to die. Their corpses strew New England today. Many of their ministers have been intellectually among the most brilliant our country has ever known, but their churches even under scholarly and brilliant ministers die, die, die. Why? Because Unitarianism presents a gospel without atoning blood, and Jesus has said and history has proven it true, *And I, if I be lifted up from the earth, will draw all men unto myself.*

Christian Science, strangely so-called for it has been truly said "is neither Christian nor scientific." It draws crowds of men and women of a certain type, men and women who have or imagine that they have physical ailments and will follow anything no matter how absurd that promises them a little relief from their real or imagined pains. It also draws crowds who wish to imagine that they have some religion without paying the price of true religion, genuine love, real self-sacrifice, and costly sympathy. But Christian Science does not draw *all* men, that is, all kinds and conditions and ranks of men. In fact, for the most part, it does not draw men at all, but women, and the alleged men it draws are for the most part women in trousers and men who see an easy way to make a living by preying upon the credulity of luckless females. No, a bloodless gospel, a gospel with a Christ, but not a Christ lifted up on a cross, does not meet the universal needs of men. It does not draw all men.

Congregationalism of late years has been sadly stained with Unitarianism. In spite of the fact that it has been an eyewitness to Unitarianism's steady decay and death, Congregationalism has largely dropped the atoning blood out of its theology, and consequently it is rapidly failing. Its once-great Andover Seminary is still great in the size of its endowment that was given for the teaching of Bible orthodoxy, but the conscienceless teachers of its bloodless theology have deliberately exploited their *damnable heresies* (2 Peter 2:1). Though still great in the number of its professors, they only graduated at their annual graduating exercises last spring just three men – one a Japanese, one a Hindu, and one an American. A theology without a crucified Savior, without the atoning blood, won't draw people. It does not meet the need. No, no, the words of our Lord are still true: *And I, if I be lifted up from the earth, will draw all men unto myself.*

And third, notice the words *draw all men* – does *all men* mean all individuals or men of all races? Did Jesus mean that every man and woman who lived on this earth would be drawn to Him, or did He mean that men of all races would be drawn to Him? The context answers the question. The Greeks, as we have seen, came to one of the apostles, Philip, and said, *We would see Jesus,* and Philip had gone and told Andrew, and Andrew and Philip had gone and told Jesus. Our Lord's ministry during His earthly life was to Jews only. With the coming of these Greeks so soon before His death, our Lord saw the foreshadowing of the coming days when by His death on the cross the barrier between Jews and Gentiles would be torn down, and all nations would have their opportunity equally with the Jews. He knew that by His atoning death on the cross, men of all nations would be drawn to Him. He did not say that He would draw every individual, but that He would draw all races of men, Greeks as well as Jews, Romans, Scythians, French, English, Germans, Japanese, Americans, and men of all nations.

He is a universal Savior, and true Christianity is a universal religion. Islam, Buddhism, Confucianism, and all other religions except Christianity are religions of a restricted application. Christianity, with a crucified Christ as its center, is a universal religion and meets the needs of all mankind. It meets the needs of the American as well as the needs of the Asian, the needs of the West as well as the needs of the Orient, the needs of the American Indian and the needs of the African American. Our Lord said, *And I, if I be lifted up from the earth, will draw all men unto myself.*

No race has ever been found anywhere on this earth to which the gospel did not appeal and whose deepest need the crucified Christ did not meet. Many years ago, Charles Darwin, the eminent English scientist, came in contact with the tribe from Tierra del Fuego in their gross degradation. He publicly declared that here was a people to whom it was vain to send missionaries, for the gospel could not do anything for them. But brave men of God went there and took the gospel to them in the power of the Holy Spirit. They demonstrated that it met the need of the Fuegians with such great results that Charles Darwin publicly admitted his mistake and became a regular subscriber to the work.

> The gospel with a crucified Christ as its center meets the needs of all conditions and classes of men as well as of all races.

The gospel with a crucified Christ as its center meets the needs of all conditions and classes of men as well as of all races. It meets the need of the millionaire and the need of the pauper; it meets the need of great men of science like James D. Dana and Lord Kelvin and the need of the man or woman who cannot read nor write; it meets the need of the king on the throne and the need of the laborer in the ditch. I have seen with my own eyes noblemen and servant girls, university deans and men who could scarcely read, prisoners in penitentiaries and leaders in moral uplift, brilliant lawyers and dull, plodding working men come under its attraction and saved by its power. But it was only because I made Christ crucified and His atoning work the center of my preaching.

In the fourth place, notice the words *unto me*. *I will draw all men unto me*. The Revised Version reads *unto myself*, and that was just what Jesus said: *And I, if I be lifted up from the earth, will draw all men unto myself*. It is not to a creed or a system of doctrine that Jesus draws men, but to a person, to Himself. That is what we need – a person, Jesus Himself. As He Himself once said, *Come unto me, all ye that labour and are heavy laden, and I will give you rest* (Matthew 11:28). Creeds and confessions of faith are all right in their place; they are of great value. The organized church is of great value; it is indispensable, and it is the most important institution in the world today. Society would soon go to rack and ruin without it; we are all under solemn obligation to God and to our fellow man to support it and belong to it. But creeds and confessions of faith cannot save; the church cannot save; the divine person, Jesus Christ, can save, and He alone. So He says, *And I, if I be lifted up from the earth, will draw all men unto myself*.

Why Christ Lifted Up Draws All Men unto Himself

But why does Christ lifted up on the cross, the crucified Christ, draw all men unto Himself? There are two reasons.

First, Christ crucified draws all men unto Himself because Christ crucified meets the first, the deepest, the greatest and most fundamental need of man. What is man's first, greatest, deepest, most fundamental need? A Savior. A Savior from what? First of all, and underlying all else, a Savior from the guilt of sin. Every man of every race has sinned. As Paul put it in Romans 3:22-24: *There is no difference: for all have sinned, and come short of the glory of God*. There is no difference between

Jew and Gentile at this point, nor is there any difference between English and German at this point; there is no difference between American and Japanese at this point, and no difference between European and Asian, no difference between the American and the African. *There is no difference: for all have sinned, and come short of the glory of God.*

Every man of every race is a sinner; *there is no difference* at this point. And every man will answer for his sin to the infinitely Holy God who rules this universe. Therefore, all men need an atoning Savior who can by His atoning death make propitiation for, and so cover up, our sins. He can thus reconcile us to this Holy God, deliver us from His awful wrath, and bring us into the glorious sunlight of His favor. And Jesus lifted up is the only atoning Savior in the universe. He alone was at the same time God and man, so He alone can make atonement for sin. He has made the perfect atonement, and God has accepted His atonement and testified to His acceptance of His atonement by raising Him from the dead.

The Lord Jesus actually meets our need; He actually meets every man's first, greatest, deepest, most fundamental need – and He alone. In all the universe no other religion but Christianity even offers an atoning Savior. Islam offers Muhammad, "The Prophet," a teacher, but not a Savior. Buddhism offers Buddha, supposedly at least a wonderful teacher, "The Light of Asia," but not an atoning Savior. Confucianism offers Confucius, a marvelous teacher far ahead of his time, but not an atoning Savior.

> No religion offers an atoning Savior, an atonement of any real character, except Christianity.

No religion offers an atoning Savior, an atonement of any real character, except Christianity. This is the radical point of difference between Christianity and every other religion in the world; yet some fool preachers are trying to eliminate this from Christianity, the very point of radical difference from all other religions. But such an emasculated Christianity will not reach the needs of men and will not draw men. It never has and it never will. The Bible and history are in agreement on this point. Jesus Christ offers Himself lifted up on the cross to redeem us from the curse of the law, by becoming a curse in our behalf. *Christ hath redeemed us from the curse of the law, being made a curse for us: for it is written, Cursed is every one that hangeth on a tree* (Galatians 3:13).

Men know their need; they may try to forget it, deny it, or drown their sense of it by drink, distraction, or wild pleasure-seeking and wild money-getting. They may listen to fake preachers in supposedly orthodox pulpits, like one who in this city declared recently that "the old sense of sin is fast disappearing," and added, "the change is for the better not for the worse." He spoke also of "imaginary and artificial sins like the sin of unbelief." He went on to say, "In this we agree with Christ," apparently not knowing enough about the Bible to know that Jesus Himself was the very one who said in John 16:8-9, *And he, when he is come, will convict the world in respect of sin, and of righteousness, and of judgment: of sin, because they believe not on me.*

But in spite of all our attempts to drown or stupefy or silence our sense of sin, our consciousness of guilt before a holy God (we all have it), like Banquo's ghost in Macbeth, will not hold down our guilt. Nothing gives the guilty conscience abiding peace except the atoning blood of Jesus Christ. And so, Christ *lifted up* draws all men unto Him, and even wicked ministers of Satan, like the preacher I have just referred to, sometimes come to their senses and flee to the real Christ, *Christ crucified*, as I hope this one may. Yes, Jesus, Jesus only, Jesus *lifted up on the cross*, Jesus crucified for our sins, making full atonement for our sins, He and He alone meets the deepest need of us all, and so His cross draws us all unto Himself.

Happy is the man or the woman who yields to that drawing. Woe to the man or woman who resists that drawing; final gloom, despondency, and despair are their lot. Oh, many men and women who have had their eyes opened to the facts and see their awful guilt, but have plunged into the deepest despair, have come to me. I pointed them to Jesus on the cross and showed them by God's Word that all their sins were laid upon Him and thus settled. They have come to Him and believed God's testimony about Him, that He had borne all their sins in His own body on the cross; they have found perfect peace and boundless joy. And that is the only way to find perfect peace and boundless joy.

Will you set out to find peace? If you do not, great gloom and utter despair await you someday in this world or in the world to come.

In my first pastorate, I tried to get a man to come to *Christ lifted up* to meet his need of pardon. Even though it was many years ago, he held to the theology that is preached as "new theology" today, and sought to still the voice of conscience and stupefy his sense of sin by denying his guilt and his need of an atoning Savior. He did not wish to listen to me or to see me. But the hour came when death was near. Cancer was eating its way through scalp and skull into his brain; then he cried to those around his dying bed, "Send for Mr. Torrey."

I hurried to his side. He was in despair. "Oh!" he said, "Dr. Tidhall tells me that I have but a short time to live; as soon as this cancer gets a little further and eats through the thin film of skull and touches the brain, I am a dead man. Tell me how to be saved." I sat down beside him and told him what to do to be saved. I tried to make as plain as I knew how the way of salvation through the *uplifted Christ,* Christ uplifted on the cross, and I think I know how to make it plain, but he had waited too long. He could not grasp it.

I stayed with him. Night came on. I said to his family, "You have been up night after night with him; I will sit with him tonight." They instructed me what to do, how to minister to him. Time after time during the night I had to go to another room to get some nourishment for him, and as I would come back into the room where he lay, from his bed in the corner I would hear his constant cry, "Oh, I wish I were a Christian. Oh, I wish I were a Christian. Oh, I wish I were a Christian." And thus, he died.

In the second place, *Christ lifted up on the cross, Christ crucified draws all men unto Him,* because lifted up there to die for us He reveals His wonderful love, and the wondrous love of the Father for us. *Hereby perceive we the love of God, because he laid down his life for us* (1 John 3:16), and *God commendeth his love toward us, in that, while we were yet sinners, Christ died for us* (Romans 5:8). There is nothing that draws men like love. Love draws all men in every climate. But no other love draws like the love of God. John 3:16, *For God so loved the world, that he gave his only begotten Son, that whosoever believeth in him should not perish, but have everlasting life,* has broken thousands of hard hearts.

One night, preaching in my own church in Minneapolis, the whole choir stayed for the after-meeting. The leading soprano was an intelligent young woman but was living a worldly life. She remained with the rest. In the after-meeting, her mother rose in the back of the church and said, "I wish you would pray for the conversion of my daughter." I did not look around but knew instinctively that her daughter's cheeks were flushing, and her eyes flashing with anger.

As soon as the meeting was dismissed, I hurried down so

that I could meet her before she left the church. As she came toward me, I held out my hand to her. She stamped her foot and with flashing eyes cried, "Mr. Torrey, my mother knows better than to do that. She knows it will only make me worse."

I said, "Sit down, Cora." She sat down, and without any argument, I opened my Bible to Isaiah 53:5. I began to read, *"But he was wounded for our transgressions, he was bruised for our iniquities: the chastisement of our peace was upon him; and with his stripes we are healed."* She burst into tears and the next night accepted Jesus Christ.

I had to go to Duluth for a few days, and when I returned, I found that this young woman was seriously ill. One morning her brother came hurrying up to my home and said that she was apparently dying, that she was unconscious and white from the loss of blood. I hastened down, and as I entered the room, she lay there with her eyes closed and with the whitest face I ever saw on one who was not actually dead. She was apparently unconscious, scarcely breathing. I knelt by her side to pray, more for the sake of the mother who stood beside the bed than for her, for I supposed that she was beyond help or hearing.

But no sooner had I finished my prayer, than in a clear, full, richly musical tone she began to pray. These were the essence of her words: "Heavenly Father, if it be Your will, raise me up that, as I have used my voice for myself and only to please myself, I may use my voice for Your glory; but if in Your wisdom You see that it is best for me not to live, I shall be glad to go to be with Christ," and she went to be with Christ.

Oh, I have seen thousands melted as I have repeated to them and shown them the picture of Christ on the cross as told in Isaiah 53:5: *But he was wounded for our transgressions, he was bruised for our iniquities: the chastisement of our peace was upon him; and with his stripes we are healed.*

A few days ago, I received a missionary magazine containing

a testimony from a person who was going to Egypt under the Egypt General Mission. This young missionary said, "When I was twelve years old, during the Torrey-Alexander meetings in 1904, I gave my heart to the Lord Jesus Christ. Dr. Torrey spoke on the text Isaiah 53:5, and he asked us to repeat the words with him, but change the word *our* to the word *my*. While repeating the text in this way, I suddenly realized, as if for the first time, that Jesus had really suffered all this for me, and there and then I gave my life to Him."

Oh, men and women, look now! See Jesus Christ lifted up on the cross; see Him hanging on that awful cross; see Him wounded for your transgressions, bruised for your iniquities, with the chastisement of your peace laid on Him. Oh, men and women living in sin, men and women rejecting Christ for the world, men and women who have looked to the lies of Christian Science, Unitarianism, and other systems that deny His atoning blood, listen! *But He was wounded for our transgressions, he was bruised for our iniquities: the chastisement of our peace was upon him; and with his stripes we are healed.* Won't you yield to that love; won't you give up your sin, give up your worldly pleasures, give up your willful errors, and accept the Savior who loves you and died for you? He was wounded for your transgressions, bruised for your iniquities, and upon Him the chastisement of your peace was laid. Accept Him right now.

Chapter 6

The Most Important Question of the Day

What shall I do then with Jesus which is called Christ? (Matthew 27:22)

If I should ask an audience today the question, "What is the most important question of the day?" I presume I would get a great variety of answers. Some of you would say that the disarmament question or the Four-Power Treaty[4] question was the most important question of the day. Some would say that the labor question was the most important question of the day. And still others would say that the prohibition question was the most important question of the day, and so on. But all these answers would be wrong. There is another question of vastly more importance than any one of these – a question upon which immeasurably more depends than upon the decision of any of these questions. That question is this: *What shall I do then with Jesus which is called Christ?* (Matthew 27:22).

---

4   The Four-Power Treaty was a treaty signed by the United States, Great Britain, France, and Japan at the Washington Naval Conference on December 13, 1921.

It is not a new question. Pontius Pilate asked it nearly nineteen hundred years ago and answered it wrongly; his earthly life went out in darkness, and his eternity was blasted. Thousands upon thousands have asked it since. Everything that is really worth having for time and for eternity depends upon a right decision of that question for each one of us. If you do the right thing with Jesus, the Christ of God, you will get everything that is worth having for time as well as for eternity, whether a right decision is given on these various other questions or not. If you do the wrong thing with Jesus, the Christ of God, you will lose everything that is worth having for time as well as for eternity, even if all these other questions are decided as they should be.

What We Get If We Do the Right Thing with Jesus Christ

In the first place, if you do the right thing with Jesus you will get the forgiveness of all your sins. The apostle Peter says in Acts 10:43, *To him give all the prophets witness, that through his name whosoever believeth in him shall receive remission of sins.* Now this statement is as plain as day, and in it God's inspired apostle declares that whosoever believes in Jesus Christ *shall receive remission of [his] sins.* If the vilest sinner on earth should come in here today and put his trust in Jesus Christ, the moment he did it, all his sins would be forgiven and blotted out.

> The forgiveness of our sins depends solely upon what we do with Jesus Christ.

The forgiveness of our sins depends solely upon what we do with Jesus Christ. It does not depend upon our prayers, our penances, or our good works. If you do the right thing with Jesus Christ, you get forgiveness of all your sins no matter what else you may or may not do. If you do the wrong thing with Jesus Christ, you will not get forgiveness of sins no matter what else you may or may not do. The same truth is put in a different way in John 3:18: *He that believeth on him is not condemned: but he that believeth not is condemned already, because he hath not believed in the name of the only begotten Son of God.*

What an unspeakable blessing the forgiveness of all your sins is. Wealth, honors, and pleasures are not so eagerly to be desired as the forgiveness of our sins. All of them together are not to be compared with the forgiveness of our sins. Forgiveness of sin brings joy anywhere it comes, whether it comes into the palace or into the prison cell. King David had wealth, honor, power, pleasures, and privileges without number, but he was not happy. Indeed, he was perfectly miserable. His own description of his condition is found in the thirty-second psalm: *When I kept silence, my bones waxed old through my roaring all the day long. For day and night thy hand was heavy upon me: my moisture is turned into the drought of summer* (Psalm 32:3-4). Then he found forgiveness of sin and in his joy he shouted, *Blessed is he whose transgression is forgiven, whose sin is covered. Blessed is the man unto whom the* Lord *imputeth not iniquity* (Psalm 32:1-2).

Down in a wretched cell in Sing Sing Prison, there was a man under a fifteen-year sentence for manslaughter. He was, of course, a very unhappy man. But there in his cell he found a Bible and read it, and through the Bible, the Holy Spirit showed him the Lord Jesus as his Savior who died in his place, and he accepted Jesus Christ as his Savior. It was in the middle of the night when he finally found the Savior through meditating on what he had read in the Word of God, and though it was in the middle of the night and in a prison cell, such joy came into his soul that he began to shout. The guard came along, rapped on his door, and told him to keep still. "I can't keep still," he shouted back, "my sins are forgiven." Yes, there is a more wonderful joy in knowing that our sins are all forgiven than there is in anything that this world has to give. And we get this forgiveness of sins by simple believing on the Lord Jesus Christ.

In the second place, you will get peace of conscience by doing the right thing with Jesus Christ. It is a blessed thing to have a conscience that does not accuse you, a conscience that has found perfect peace. It is an awful thing to have a conscience that does accuse. It is the greatest misery on earth. It drives many men and many women to suicide. Oh, in what agony of mind men and women have come to me from different ranks of society because of an accusing conscience. And there are many who never unburden their hearts to others and are in misery from the same cause. There are men and women who spend days and nights of misery because of an accusing conscience. You might try to drown the voice of conscience in many ways, but you will fail utterly. You might try to drown the voice of conscience in pleasure and debauchery. You might try to drown the voice of conscience in business or in drink and drugs, or in other ways; but you do not succeed. You never will succeed.

One who perhaps knows as much about the life of the Movie Colony in Hollywood[5] as anyone else told a friend of mine a few weeks ago of two of the leading stars in the movie world, two women whose names are constantly in the daily papers and who are admired and envied by thousands, but they were the hopeless slaves of drugs. All over this land people are considered gifted, and others look on in envy, but they are trying to silence the voice of conscience with drugs. But no one ever yet found real peace in that way, and no one ever will. Jesus Christ alone can give the guilty conscience peace.

In Romans 5:1, through the apostle Paul, God put it in this way: *Being justified by faith, we have peace with God through our Lord Jesus Christ.* Do the right thing with Jesus Christ, and you will get true peace of conscience – deep, abiding peace, perfect

---

5   The Movie Colony is a neighborhood in Palm Springs, California, named after the many movie stars who owned homes there between the 1930s and 1960s.

peace. As Isaiah said, *Thou wilt keep him in perfect peace, whose mind is stayed on thee: because he trusteth in thee* (Isaiah 26:3). But do the wrong thing with Jesus Christ, and you cannot find peace of conscience in this world or in the next, no matter what else you may do to try to get peace.

I was dealing once in my office with a woman who told me that she had been in a perfect hell from an accusing conscience for fourteen years. I pointed her to Jesus Christ. I showed her from God's Word how all her sins had been laid upon Jesus Christ. She believed it. She took God's Word for it, and she put her trust in Him as her atoning Savior. After fourteen years of agony, of hell on earth, she went out from my office that day with a radiant countenance, for she had found peace of conscience in the only way in which peace of conscience can ever be found by anybody – through her Lord Jesus Christ. And that joy continues until this day.

In the third place, you will get deliverance from the power of sin by doing the right thing with Jesus Christ. It is a dreadful thing to be in the power of sin. There is no other slavery so binding, so degrading, and so crushing as the slavery of sin. We all know what a dreadful thing it is to be in the power of some sins. We all know, for example, what an awful thing it is to be in the power of strong drink. We know what an awful thing it is to be in the power of morphine, cocaine, or some other kind of drug. Many of us know personally or through stories of others, distressing and agonizing stories, what an awful thing it is to be in the power of lust. How many men have come to me in despair this past year and told the story of their dreadful slavery. It is an awful thing to be in the power of sin of any kind.

There is, however, a way to get free. There is a way by which any man or woman who is the slave of any sin of any kind can get instantaneous and complete deliverance from the power of that sin. There is only one way. That way is by doing the right thing with Jesus Christ.

You cannot get out of sin's power unless you do the right thing with Jesus Christ. You may get free from some bad habits. You may, for example, give up drinking without the help of Christ, though very few do; but whether you do or do not, you will not get out of sin's grip; you will simply turn from one sin to another. Christ alone can save you from sin's power. I could stand here by the hour and tell you of men and women I have personally known, men and women as completely enslaved by sin in one form or another as any man or woman who ever walked the earth, whom the Lord Jesus Christ has set free when they did the right thing with Him.

In the fourth place, you will get great joy by doing the right thing with Jesus Christ. The apostle Peter says in 1 Peter 1:8, *On whom, though now ye see him not, yet believing, ye rejoice greatly with joy unspeakable and full of glory.* You can get *joy unspeakable and full of glory* by doing the right thing with Jesus Christ. You cannot get *joy unspeakable and full of glory* in any other way.

You know happy people, of course, who are not Christians, but you do not know anyone who is not a Christian who has *joy unspeakable and full of glory.* You do not know anyone who is not a Christian who has the deep, constant, satisfying, and overflowing joy that those men and women have who are not merely nominal Christians but real Christians. Those men and women have fully accepted Christ as their personal Savior and are really trusting God for the forgiveness of all their sins, because they fully believe God's testimony concerning Jesus Christ having borne every one of their sins when He died on the cross. Thus, they have fully settled their sins forever and have without reservation surrendered the entire control of their thoughts and lives to Jesus Christ. They have confessed Jesus Christ as their Lord before the world in every reasonable opportunity they get, and have watched for every opportunity to lead others to Christ. They are serving Jesus Christ with all their strength every day.

Do the right thing with Jesus Christ and you get this wonderful joy. Reject Jesus Christ and you lose it. How foolish men and women are! Many men today are rejecting Christ because they think they will lose joy if they take Christ. Are you blind, men? Do you not see that those who have taken Christ really are happier than you are? Do you not see that many Christians are happier in poverty than skeptics and worldly persons are in wealth? Are you deaf, women? Have you not heard many from all ranks of society, whose word you must believe, testify that they have found a joy since they took Christ that they never dreamed of in the world?

I do not think many of you could tell me much that I do not know about this world's joys. I have tasted most of them, but I never knew *joy unspeakable and full of glory* until I took Jesus Christ. I do now. My every day is full of joy. I have perplexities; I have annoyances; I have experiences that could easily prove exasperating. I have burdens of many kinds; I have what may appear to be great losses; I have things said to me and written to me and said and printed about me that would cut to the quick if I did not know the Lord Jesus. But through it all, every day is unspeakably happy.

Not so long ago I had more things come to me that might have caused grief and anxiety and worry and heartache and deep sorrow than in almost any other week of my life, but it was a radiantly happy week. Why? Simply because of what Jesus Christ is to me, as my Lord and my Savior.

In the fifth place, if you do the right thing with Jesus Christ you will get eternal life. Eternal life! What a wonderful phrase that is – eternal life. Life that never ends. Life that knows no death. Life of unutterable beauty and dignity and honor and glory and rapture! Life that is endless in its duration and perfect in its quality. Life like the life of God Himself. ETERNAL LIFE! What can the world offer in comparison with that? What is the wealth of a John D. Rockefeller or a Henry Ford compared with eternal life? I would rather be a penniless pauper all my days, living in destitution, hunger, rags, and cold, and have eternal life, than to roll in wealth all my days with all that wealth can buy but not have eternal life. I have no envy for the rich. No, I know their lives and hearts too well. I have often a greater pity for them than for the poor, for they are often more to be pitied than the poor. The life of the average millionaire is a sad, sad life.

What is the wisdom of an Edison or of the world's greatest scientist or philosopher compared with eternal life? What are the honors of a great general or a mighty ruler of men compared with eternal life? What are the pleasures of the most successful enthusiast of pleasure compared with eternal life? Put all that the world has, absolutely everything the world can give, into one pan of the scales. Put eternal life into the other pan. See the world's side go up. It is lighter than the smallest dust on the balance in comparison with eternal life. Eternal life! Oh, who can fathom all the depth of meaning that there is in these two wondrous words?

> Put all that the world has into one pan of the scales. Put eternal life into the other pan. See the world's side go up.

And you get it by simply doing the right thing with Jesus Christ. Do the right thing with Jesus Christ and you get eternal life. Do the wrong thing with Jesus Christ and you lose eternal life. Notice God's own Word about that: *He that believeth on the*

Son hath everlasting life: and he that believeth not the Son shall not see life; but the wrath of God abideth on him (John 3:36).

Again, God's Word says, *And the witness is this, that God gave unto us eternal life, and this life is in his Son. He that hath the Son hath the life; he that hath not the Son of God hath not the life* (1 John 5:11-12).

Are you going to do the right thing with Jesus Christ today and get eternal life, or are you going to do the wrong thing with Jesus Christ and forever lose eternal life?

But there is something even better than eternal life that you get by doing the right thing with Jesus Christ. By doing the right thing with Jesus Christ, you become a child of God, an heir of God, and a joint heir with Jesus Christ. We read in God's own Word in John 1:12: *As many as received him, to them gave he the right to become children of God, even to them that believe on his name.* And in Romans 8:17 we read: *If children, then heirs; heirs of God, and joint-heirs with Christ.*

Just think of that for a moment – a child of God, an heir of God, and a joint heir (or fellow heir) with Jesus Christ. We have heard these words very often, but have we ever stopped to weigh their meaning and take in their wondrous importance? A child of God! Think of it! God the infinite One, God the Creator of all things, God to whom the whole race of men and the whole company of angels are as nothing – and we are to become His children and His heirs. We are to be heirs of all that this infinite God is and all that this infinite God has. It almost staggers the mind to try to think of it. That is what is open to each one of us. That is what is open to you and open to me by just doing the right thing with Jesus Christ.

One day years ago, I met the son and heir of one of the richest men in the whole world, and he invited me to dinner. As I sat and talked with him, it seemed to me as if it might be in some respects a fine thing to be the son and heir of the richest millionaire on earth. But that is nothing, just nothing at all compared to being a child of God, an heir of God and fellow heir with Jesus Christ. That is what is open to us, to each one of us; but it can be obtained in only one way – by doing the right thing with Jesus Christ. Do the right thing with Jesus Christ, and in a moment you become a child of God, an heir of God and fellow heir with Jesus Christ. Read God's own statement about it again: *As many as received him, to them gave he the right to become children of God, even to them that believe on his name* (John 1:12).

Do the wrong thing with Jesus Christ, and you lose forever your chance of becoming a child of God, an heir of God, and a fellow heir with Jesus Christ. Oh, what a loss that is! The loss of untold wealth, the loss of earth's greatest honors, and the loss of dearest friends is nothing in comparison with the loss of becoming a child of God, an heir of God, and a fellow heir with Jesus Christ. That is the awful cost of doing the wrong thing with Jesus Christ. We see then something of what we gain by doing the right thing with Jesus Christ, and something of what we lose by doing the wrong thing with Jesus Christ. By doing the right thing with Jesus Christ, we gain forgiveness of all our sins. By doing the right thing with Jesus Christ, we gain peace of conscience. By doing the right thing with Jesus Christ, we gain deliverance from sin's power. By doing the right thing with Jesus Christ, we gain *joy unspeakable and full of glory.* By doing the right thing with Jesus Christ, we gain eternal life. By doing the right thing with Jesus Christ, we become children of God, heirs of God, and fellow heirs with Jesus Christ. Is it not evident, then, that the most important question of this day and of all days is, *What shall I do then with Jesus which is called Christ?*

But what will *you* do with Him? Will *you* do the right thing with Him, or will *you* do the wrong thing with Him? Will *you* do the right thing and gain all or will *you* do the wrong thing and lose all? I put the question to each individual reader: What will *you* do with Jesus? It does not matter whether you are a church member or not, I put the question to you: What will *you* do with Jesus? I put the question to the most worldly man or woman as well as to the most religious: *What will you do with Jesus who is called Christ?* I put the question to the one who is most sunken in sin, for there is hope for you of getting all these things if you do the right thing with Jesus Christ, just as much as there is for the most moral, upright, and highly respected man or woman here: *What then will you do with Jesus which is called Christ?* Of each one of you I ask, Will *you* do the right thing with Jesus Christ, or will *you* do the wrong thing with Jesus Christ?

But there is something better than anything I have mentioned yet that depends entirely upon what you do with Jesus Christ. If you do the right thing *with Jesus Christ,* then some day you will become just like Him. Read what God says: *Behold what manner of love the Father hath bestowed upon us, that we should be called children of God: and such we are. . . . Beloved, now are we children of God, and it is not yet made manifest what we shall be. We know that, if he shall be manifested, we shall be like him; for we shall see him even as he is* (1 John 3:1-2).

"What?" someone will say. "Can I become like Jesus Christ?" Yes, even you can become just like Jesus Christ. Think of it! You and I with all our present failings, shortcomings, meanness, and pettiness that others see clearly, for they stick out all over us. They generally stick out most conspicuously upon those of us who have the best opinion of ourselves. But even we can become just like Him, like Him in every perfection and glory of His matchless, faultless, glorious, divine character. Yes, and we can be like Him in the glory of His outward appearance too. It is written in the Word of God: *For our citizenship is in heaven; from whence also we wait for a Saviour, the Lord Jesus Christ: who shall fashion anew the body of our humiliation, that it may be conformed to the body of his glory, according to the working whereby he is able even to subject all things unto himself* (Philippians 3:20-21).

And how can we become just like Him? By doing the right thing with Jesus Christ.

The Right Thing to Do with Jesus Christ

But what is the right thing to do with Jesus Christ?

First, the right thing to do with Jesus Christ is to receive Him as your Savior. This is evident from the verse that we have quoted already a number of times, John 1:12: *As many as received him, to them gave he the right to become children of God, even to them that believe on his name.* He died for your sins. *All we like sheep have gone astray; we have turned every one to his own way; and the* LORD *hath laid on him the iniquity of us all* (Isaiah 53:6).

Will you accept Him as your sin-bearer? Will you say, "Oh God, I believe what Your Word says about Jesus Christ. I believe He bore my sins in His own body on the cross. I believe every one of my sins was laid upon Him and settled fully and forever when He died on the cross in my place. And I now take Him as my sin-bearer. Forgive all my sins for Jesus Christ's sake."

> Take Him not only as your Savior from the guilt of sin but also take Him as your Savior from the power of sin.

Take Him not only as your Savior from the guilt of sin but also take Him as your Savior from the power of sin. He not only died to make atonement for your sins, He also rose again, and He lives today to set you free from the power of sin and to make intercession for you (Hebrews 7:25). Will you take Him today as your deliverer from the power of sin? Will you come to this risen and mighty Lord Jesus with all your weakness and sins and trust Him to set you free? That is the right thing to do with Jesus Christ: just take Him as your Savior, your crucified Savior from the guilt of sin and your risen Savior from the power of sin.

The next right thing to do with Jesus is to let Him into your heart. *Behold, I stand at the door, and knock: if any man hear my voice, and open the door, I will come in to him, and will sup with him, and he with me* (Revelation 3:20). Jesus is standing at the door of every heart. He is knocking at the door of every heart. Will you open the door and let Him in? Who will? Who will say, "Lord Jesus, come in. Come in and reign."

The next right thing to do with Jesus is to enthrone Him in your heart. He is the Christ, God's anointed King, because God has made Him so. As Peter said on the day of Pentecost, *God hath made him both Lord and Christ, this Jesus whom ye crucified* (Acts 2:36). Will you enthrone Him as King in your heart? Will you say honestly to Him, "Lord Jesus, take the throne of my heart and live and reign there supreme." Who will do it?

Once more, the right thing to do with Jesus Christ is to confess Him before the world as your Lord and Master. He says in Matthew 10:32-33, *Every one therefore who shall confess me before men, him will I also confess before my Father which is in heaven. But whosoever shall deny me before men, him will I also deny before my Father which is in heaven.* And Paul says in Romans 10:9-10, *If thou shalt confess with thy mouth Jesus as Lord, and shalt believe in thy heart that God raised him from the dead, thou shalt be saved: for with the heart man believeth unto righteousness; and with the mouth confession is made unto salvation.* Who will do it?

There is one more right thing to do with Jesus. What is it? Go tell others about Him after you have taken Him as your

Savior, after you have let Him into your heart, enthroned Him as King, and confessed Him before the world as your Lord.

When Jesus was here on earth, He cast a legion of demons out of a wretched man who was under their control. The condition of that man before he met Jesus was awful beyond description, but the condition of that man after he met Jesus was glorious beyond description. And that man naturally wanted to go with Jesus wherever He went. But Jesus said, *Return to thy house, and declare how great things God hath done for thee. And he went his way, publishing throughout the whole city how great things Jesus had done for him* (Luke 8:38-39). Oh, if you have taken Jesus, go tell everyone you can about Him and bring everyone you can to Him.

These are the right things to do with Jesus. Who will do them today and gain all that is worth having for time and for eternity? Who will take Him as their Savior? Who will listen to His voice and let Him into his heart? Who will enthrone Him in his heart as King? Who will begin the confession of Him as his Lord?

Chapter 7

Great Things and How Anyone Can Get Them

All things are yours. (1 Corinthians 3:21)

You will find my text in 1 Corinthians 3:21: *All things are yours.* That text stirs the blood. I pity any man who is not stirred to the very depths of his being by an utterance of God like that – *All things are yours.* There are many who think that only a few men can ever attain great things, that the great mass of men must rest content with small things of little account. That is not so. The very greatest things, indeed, everything that is of infinite and eternal value, is open to all men. There is not a man or woman here who cannot have great things, the very greatest things, those things which are of most priceless worth. Certainly, if anyone will become a member of that class of people to whom God, in our text, makes the marvelous promise – *All things are yours* – he can have the very greatest things, those things which are of most priceless value.

Great Joy

First of all, anyone can have great joy. When Christ was born at Bethlehem, an angel came down from heaven and proclaimed, *Behold, I bring you good tidings of great joy, which shall be to all people. For unto you is born this day in the city of David a Saviour, which is Christ the Lord* (Luke 2:10-11). The birth of Jesus, the Christ of God, into this world brought great joy into the world. The reception of Jesus Christ as Savior and Lord by the individual man or woman brings great joy into the heart of that man or woman. No matter who the man or woman may be who receives Jesus Christ, they will find joy, great joy *in Him*. The highest form of joy known to man is joy in the Lord Jesus. The Lord Jesus fills every heart into which He is admitted with boundless joy. One may be very gloomy and despondent by nature, but if he really receives Jesus Christ, he will find great joy.

I recall a man who I think was one of the gloomiest men I ever met. He had one of those despondent, despairing faces that make you shudder. I dreaded to have him approach me. The man had at one time been the inmate of an insane asylum where he was sent for severe depression, and he looked and acted as if he ought to still be there. It was my privilege to point that man to Jesus Christ. He did not accept Jesus Christ in a day. I dealt with him day after day for quite a while, and he seemed so deeply immersed in his gloom that the light could not penetrate his darkened heart. It seemed as if he never would see the truth and accept the Lord Jesus. He was one of the most discouraging men with whom I have ever dealt. But he kept coming back to me, and at last, by the power of the Holy Spirit, the light broke in upon his darkened heart, and he received Jesus Christ. He became at once one of the brightest, happiest men I ever knew, as well as one of the most faithful and effective Christian workers.

I met another man who had made a shipwreck of his life. He belonged to a good family; he was a man of unusual ability and well educated, but he had gone wrong and had thrown away his life in sin. The night I first met him he was a wanderer on the face of the earth, hundreds of miles from home, money gone, friends gone, manhood gone, and seemingly everything worthwhile gone. He came to me at the close of a service I was conducting and asked me if I thought there was any hope for a man like him. I told him, "Yes," and that I knew that there was. I pointed him to the Lord Jesus, and he took Him that night and became a very happy man. That was years ago, but for many years, every now and then, I got a letter from him telling me of his great joy. Today he is happy indeed, for he is with Christ in glory.

No one ever really took Jesus Christ, rich or poor, learned or ignorant, moral or vicious, honest or criminal, of any nation or character, who did not find great joy. God has provided great joy for everyone in Jesus Christ. I know a man at the present time who is in San Quentin for murder, but in San Quentin where he has already been for some years, he was led to accept the Lord Jesus Christ. His letters, some of which his father lets me see, are among the most joyous letters and more full of Jesus Christ than any letters I have ever seen.

If anyone does not have great joy, it is wholly his own fault. No one can rob another of his joy if his joy is really in Jesus Christ. Men may rob you of your money; they may rob you of your good name; they may rob you of your friends, but they cannot rob you of your joy, if it really is in the Lord Jesus.

I met a woman in Chicago many years ago. She was most wretched. Great misfortunes had come into her life. She had been defrauded of her money. She had been robbed of her husband

and his love. Her soul was bitter. She had a hard, sour face – one of the hardest faces I ever saw. I spoke to her of Jesus Christ. She would not listen. She hated the one who had wronged her and longed to get even; she would not listen to the story of the love of God. She said God did not love her, or He would never have permitted her to suffer what she had suffered.

I met the same woman again in the Moody Church some years later. Again, I spoke to her of Jesus Christ and of God's love. This time she professed to be an infidel. I knew she was lying to me and told her so; I recalled her story as she had told it to me several years before. She assumed that I had forgotten her, so she had ventured on this new story that she was an infidel. But she was still hard and bitter.

A year or two later I met her again. Again, I spoke to her of Jesus Christ, and this time she broke down and accepted Him. Immediately her life was changed. Instead of bitterness, she found great joy at once. I met her again sometime later. She had been very sick but was still rejoicing in Jesus Christ and longing to tell others of this wonderful Savior and the joy He brings into the hearts of those who accept Him.

I was once sitting in my office in Minneapolis, and a woman with a very hard face came in. She approached my desk and said, "Do you send missionaries to talk with people who are dying?"

"Yes," I replied.

"Well, there is a woman dying at my house," and she gave me the street and number. "I wish you would send a missionary around to talk to her."

I judged from the woman's appearance the kind of place it must be and the kind of woman it must be who was dying. In a little while, two women missionaries came in. I said to them, "There is a woman dying at such and such a street and number. Will you go and talk with her? I think it is a wicked place and the woman has lived a life of sin."

The two missionaries went aside and prayed, and then they went to this house. It was as I had suspected – a den of infamy. The dying woman was a woman who had made the worst shipwreck of life that a woman can make. They told the dying woman of Jesus Christ and His death for her upon the cross of Calvary and how He had made full atonement for all her sins. And then she received Jesus Christ and great joy at once came into the heart which sin had so darkened. When the missionaries came back, I asked them, "Did she accept Jesus Christ?"

"Yes," they said, "but that is not all, Mr. Torrey. Though she was dying of an incurable disease that no physician could heal, we were led to kneel down and pray that God would not only save her soul but would also heal her body. God heard our prayer, and she is healed." The woman was beyond any human physician's skill, but these missionaries had been given faith to pray for her recovery from an incurable and loathsome disease.

> There is great joy for everybody, if they will only seek it in God's way.

God had heard their prayer. She got up from that bed a saved, happy, and well woman. Years afterward, when I had moved to Chicago, one of these two missionaries came to Chicago to study at the Moody Bible Institute. This woman heard that the missionary was coming and came to her and told her to bring me a message of her joy in the Lord.

Oh, there is great joy for everybody, if they will only seek it in God's way. Anyone can have it. We are told in Acts 8:8 that when Samaria received the truth regarding the Lord Jesus Christ, *there was great joy in that city*. If anyone will receive the truth regarding Jesus Christ and receive Jesus Christ Himself into their heart, there will be *great joy* in that heart.

Great Peace

But there is another great thing anyone can have. You can have great peace. Peace and joy are closely related, but they are not the same thing by any means. But they are to be obtained in much the same way. If we accept Jesus Christ, trust in Him, and obey His Word, we shall have great peace as well as great joy. Paul says in Philippians 4:6-7, *In nothing be anxious; but in everything by prayer and supplication with thanksgiving let your requests be made known unto God. And the peace of God, which passeth all understanding, shall guard your hearts and your thoughts in Christ Jesus.*

And the experience of thousands and tens of thousands of people proves this promise that God made through Paul to be absolutely true.

Think of that! *The peace of God, which passeth all understanding*! Isn't that a great peace? It is infinite peace, *the peace of God* – not only the peace which God gives, but also the deep, infinite peace that there is in the heart of God Himself. And it is for anyone who desires it. Your heart may be tempest-tossed tonight. Your heart may be a raging sea of doubts, fears, anxieties, unsatisfied desires, and passions. But there is peace for you, great peace, perfect peace, *the peace of God, which passeth all understanding.*

I wonder if there was ever a more tempestuous soul than that of Saul of Tarsus. He breathed an atmosphere of storm, passion, and hatred. He was *breathing out* [or, to translate more exactly, *breathed in*] *threatenings and slaughter against the disciples of the Lord* (Acts 9:1). But that stormy soul found such peace in Jesus Christ and such peace through the power of the Holy Spirit whom Jesus Christ gives to all those who receive Him. Even in jail at Philippi at midnight, when his back was torn and bleeding from the stripes he had just received, we find him singing praises to God (Acts 16:23-25). And later, in prison at Rome, awaiting a sentence of death, no ruffle of anxiety or fear disturbs the deep calm of his soul. It was at that time he uttered such words as these: *Rejoice in the Lord always: and again I say, Rejoice* (Philippians 4:4). And a little further on he writes the words I just quoted: *In nothing be anxious; but in everything by prayer and supplication with thanksgiving let your requests be made known unto God. And the peace of God, which passeth all understanding, shall guard your hearts and your thoughts in Christ Jesus.*

And a little further on he says again, I have learned, in whatsoever state I am, therein to be content (Philippians 4:11). And two verses still further on he says, I can do all things in *h*im that strengtheneth me (Philippians 4:13). Yes, everyone can have great peace, abiding peace, abounding peace, never-failing peace, the peace of God, which passeth all understanding. On the night before His crucifixion in His farewell words to His disciples and to all who would become disciples in later years, Jesus said, Peace I leave with you; my peace I give unto you: not as the world giveth, give I unto you. Let not your heart be troubled, neither let it be fearful (John 14:27).

A Great Position

There is another great thing anyone can have, and that is a great position. We have a way of thinking that the great positions are only for a very select few. That is a great mistake. The greatest and grandest and most glorious of all positions is for anyone who will have it. Very few can ever be president of the United States. Very few can become United States senators or members of Congress. Very, very few can ever become kings or emperors. But there is a position far higher than that of congressman or senator, or president of the United States, or king or emperor, that is open to any one of us.

In John 1:12 you will find out what that position is. It says, *As many as received him, to them gave he the right to become children of God, even to them that believe on his name.* To be a child of God is surely to occupy a higher position than to be an earthly president, prince, king, or emperor. What is any earthly monarch compared to the King of Kings and the Lord of Lords? The greatest and most potent monarch on this earth looks like a gnat when compared with the infinite, eternal God, who created all things seen and unseen. The greatest earthly throne is but a toadstool compared with the throne of God. And the position of becoming God's child and God's heir is open to anyone who desires it in his heart.

One day it was my fortune to meet, by accident, a real live king. I was not looking for him, and he certainly was not looking for me. I was coming down the hall of the university at Leipzig all alone, and I saw a man coming up the stairway all alone. I instantly recognized him as the king of Saxony. I uncovered my head and bowed respectfully as we passed one another, and he bowed back with a smile, very courteously and very pleasantly. And I had met a king, and he had met – what had he met? He had met a free American citizen, but he had met something more than that; he had met a child of God. To be a child of God is to hold a far higher position than to be a king. And this position is open to anyone who wishes to fill it. *As many as received him, to them gave he the right to become children of God, even to them that believe on his name.* Think of it! Any man or woman can become a child of God. Yes, anyone.

But some of you will decline that great honor. Why? Because you would rather have some disgusting sin or some contemptible sin in your life than to become a child of God. Or you would rather have the silly satisfaction of calling yourself a skeptic and therefore imagining yourself very brainy and an independent thinker than to become a child of God. Or you are not willing to endure the world's sneers, and you would rather have this fool world's praise than to be even a child of God. Oh, for what cheap trinkets we trade this great honor of becoming children of God! What pitiful fools we are. I did it for years myself. I thank our wondrous God that He had mercy upon me, had patience with me, and at last brought me to my senses.

A Great Hope

There is another great thing that anyone can have, and that is a great hope. Paul describes this great hope. He says in Titus 1:2, *In hope of eternal life, which God, who cannot lie, promised.* What a hope that is: *hope of eternal life!* The world has nothing to match against that. The very best the world can give cannot last more than eighty, ninety, or a hundred years at the longest. We say this world has been good to Rockefeller, for it has given him several hundred millions of dollars, or it may be a billion. But for how long? For but a very little while. The poorest living newsboy on the streets of this city will be richer than Rockefeller in this world's wealth in a very few years. This world's hopes are poor things, for upon them all is written: "For a few days only."

One day, quite a while ago, the newspapers contained glowing accounts of the magnificent gifts of gold and precious stones presented to two young people who were to be married. The man was the son of one of America's richest millionaires, and the woman was the daughter of a multimillionaire. But in a very few years, they will leave all these costly gifts, all these diamonds and pearls and all this gold. But the one who will believe on Jesus Christ gets a hope that is indeed great – eternal life – life divine in its quality, endless in its duration, the very life of God Himself. Years roll on; the eternal life still lasts. Centuries fly by; the eternal life still lasts. Ages and ages sweep on in endless procession, but the eternal life is just beginning. Ah, eternal life! That is something worthwhile.

To me there is a growing charm in these words – *eternal life*. In former years I did not think much of them. The present life seemed fair and long and very alluring. But lately, I have seen one thing after another end; I have seen vast fortunes crumble, and one great man after another pass into oblivion and someone else come on and take his place. I have seen not only vast fortunes but also mighty kings and even vast empires collapse and vanish. I have seen the stamp of impermanence and decay upon everything earthly. I have felt an ever-increasing pity for the poor fools who live for the present fleeting world, and an increasing joy in these great words – *eternal life*.

In hope of eternal life – that is indeed a hope worth having. And anyone can have it. The poorest can have it as well as the richest. The weakest can have it as well as the strongest. The most sinful can have it as well as the holiest. The great, the glorious hope of life eternal is open to all.

A Great Inheritance

Then there is another great thing that is open to all, and that is a great inheritance. Peter describes this inheritance in this way: *An inheritance incorruptible, and undefiled, and that fadeth not away, reserved in heaven* (1 Peter 1:4). Now that cannot be said about any earthly inheritance. What earthly inheritance is incorruptible? The hand of decay is upon every earthly inheritance. What earthly inheritance is undefiled? My, how dirty most great earthly inheritances are. What earthly inheritance *fadeth not away*? They are fading, every last one. The fool son or grandson of the shrewdest millionaire is likely to wind up in jail, and the inheritance disappears entirely in almost every case as soon as the owner of it dies.

In Romans 8:16-17 Paul describes this great inheritance that any one of us can get in a still more remarkable way: *The Spirit himself beareth witness with our spirit, that we are children of God: and if children, then heirs; heirs of God, and joint-heirs with Christ.* Think of that for a moment, please. *Heirs of God!* Heirs of all God's infinite wealth, joy, and glory, and *joint-heirs* [fellow heirs, co-heirs] *with Christ,* heirs in the way in which Jesus Christ is heir, and to the extent to which Jesus Christ is an heir. Co-heirs with Him in whom dwelt *all the fulness of the Godhead bodily* (Colossians 2:9), and who was, therefore, the *heir of all things* (Hebrews 1:2).

In that same way the one who receives Jesus Christ becomes an heir of God. Look out upon the whole earth with all its wealth and say, "This all belongs to God, and I am His child and His heir, and therefore I am heir of all this." Look up at the stars, those great, immeasurable, incomprehensible, overwhelmingly stupendous worlds of light and splendor and bewildering magnitude and majesty, and say, "I am an heir of all these." Think of the infinite wisdom, infinite joy, and infinite glory of the Deity and say, "I am His child. Therefore, all this is my inheritance. There is absolutely no limit to what is open to me." Millionaire? That is nothing. Billionaire? That is still nothing. I am an heir of God, a co-heir with Jesus Christ! It fairly makes one's head swim just to think of it. This inheritance is open to anyone. Take, for example, some washerwoman. This inheritance is open to her. Or some laboring man. This inheritance is open to him. Or an ex-convict. This inheritance is open to him. Or men and women who have squandered their lives. This inheritance is open to them.

One night in Birmingham, England, upon going onto the platform in Bingley Hall, I received a note from a young woman. She asked me to pray for her brother whom she said had squandered two fortunes and had just returned from India where he had squandered a third. I read the note from the platform, and the audience joined me in prayer for this man. Though we did not know it, miles away in Worcester, while we prayed, that man was seated by a table with a loaded revolver, preparing to take his own life. But God heard our prayer, and he was converted and saved as he sat by that table, just within a few minutes of hell. He had thrown away three inheritances, but he received an inheritance that night to which all three together were as nothing.

There are poor men; there are rich men. There are good men; there are bad men. But this inheritance is open to one and all without distinction. Peter puts it this way: *An inheritance incorruptible, and undefiled, and that fadeth not away, reserved in heaven for you.* For whom? *For you, who are kept by the power of God through faith unto salvation ready to be revealed in the last time.* Do you take in the force of these words? This inheritance is for anyone who believes on Jesus Christ; he is therefore kept not by his own power but by the power of God. He is kept unto that complete salvation of spirit, soul, and body that is to be made manifest in the last time. That, then, is all one has to do to get this great inheritance – just place faith in Jesus Christ and be *kept by the power of God through faith unto [that glorious, infinite] salvation ready to be revealed in the last time.* Anyone can do that, and therefore anyone can get this inheritance.

We see, then, that there is for us all, for anyone who will have them, a great joy, a great peace, a great position, a great hope, and a great inheritance. Do you want these five great things? I put the question to each one of you. Do you want these five great things? You can have them. Take Jesus Christ as your Savior and surrender to Him as your Lord; confess Him as such before the world, and these five great things become yours. Do that and you will get them all. Oh, how can any one of you refuse to do it? How can you hesitate to do it? If I should take a bushel basket full of large diamonds of the finest quality and make it known that anyone who wished could have one, would you hesitate? There might be some friend near you to laugh at you, but you would come just the same. Well, I am setting out something infinitely better than a basket full of fine diamonds. I set forth a great peace; I set forth here a great joy; I set forth a great position; I set forth a great honor; I set forth here a great hope; I set forth here a great inheritance, and I say on the authority of God, who cannot lie, "Come up and help yourself." How many of you will?

Chapter 8

Noah and the Ark

And the LORD *said unto Noah, Come thou and all thy house into the ark.* (Genesis 7:1)

Noah was one of the most remarkable men in the world's history. He stands out absolutely alone of all the men of his day. He was the one man whom God chose out of the whole human race then living to be the head of a new race. The story of the flood is a most amazing one, so unusual, indeed, that one's first impulse is to question its historicity. But it has abundant confirmation even outside the Bible. Legends of a universal flood are found nearly everywhere that men are found. The cuneiform tablets of Central Asia, the Bhagavatas of ancient India, and the legend of Deucalion in Greece present well-documented stories of the flood. The traditions of the Cree Indians in the North and of the natives of Orinoco in the South and of China on the East also picture a great flood. Mexico in the Southwest, Scandinavia in the far north, and the ancient Celts all contain accounts of such a flood. The three great branches of the human race, the Turanians, Semites, and Aryans, all have it. So it is evident that this extraordinary story of the flood has abundant historical confirmation outside of the very plain and very full and very precise statements of the Bible.

But more important than all this is that the Old Testament story has the endorsement of Jesus Christ. You cannot doubt the truth of the story of the flood as recorded in the book of Genesis without discrediting Jesus Christ. If this story is not true, then Jesus Christ was a fool, for He expressed in the most unmistakable terms His belief in the truth of the story. Yes, if this story is not true, Jesus Christ was worse than a fool – He was a fraud. He claimed to be a teacher sent from God, who spoke the very words of God, and if the story of the flood is not true, if it is not accurate history, then Jesus accepted an idle tale as true history. Then His claim to be a teacher sent from God, who spoke the very words of God, was false, and He was a gross impostor.

Not only the credibility but also the honor of Jesus Christ are involved in the truthfulness and accuracy of this Old Testament story of the flood. But Jesus Christ's claims to have been a teacher sent from God who spoke the very words of God are abundantly substantiated. They are so abundantly substantiated that no one can thoroughly and candidly study the conclusive proofs of the truth of His claims and not believe in them. Consequently, he must believe in the truth of the story of the flood, which Jesus Christ so explicitly and fully endorsed.

> Not only the credibility but also the honor of Jesus Christ are involved in the truthfulness of the story of the flood.

So it is certain that the story of the flood as recorded in the book of Genesis is true history. It is true that the world was swept away in judgment by a flood, and Noah and his family, eight persons in all, alone were saved of all members of the

Adamic race then living on the earth. Why was Noah saved? The Bible tells us.

Noah Was Saved by Grace

In the first place, Noah was saved because he found grace in the sight of the Lord. God's own statement is, *Noah found grace in the eyes of the* LORD (Genesis 6:8). Noah was not necessarily saved because he deserved to be saved. He was "saved by grace." He was not saved because he was sinless. It is true that he was righteous; Genesis 7:1 says so. Hebrews 11:7 tells us that Noah's righteousness was a righteousness of faith. The exact words are *Noah, . . . became heir of the righteousness which is according to faith* (Hebrews 11:7).

Noah's righteousness was the kind of righteousness that is open to every one of us, even open to the vilest sinner on earth. Noah was a sinner. He was not sinless; he was far from it. He was far from perfect; he got drunk even after the flood and his wonderful deliverance (Genesis 9:21). Of course, he had more of an excuse for getting drunk than you or I would have today. He did not understand the effects of alcohol as fully as we do, but he surely must have known that it was not right to get drunk. He was a sinner saved by grace.

So must we be sinners saved by grace if we are saved at all, and we all can be saved in that way; not one of us can be saved in any other way. God's Word is as plain as day on that point, and universal experience confirms God's Word on this point. God says, There is no difference: for all have sinned, *and come short of the glory of God; being justified freely by his grace through the redemption that is in Christ Jesus* (Romans 3:22-24).

And He says again, *For by grace have ye been saved through faith; and that not of yourselves: it is the gift of God* (Ephesians 2:8).

Noah Was Saved by Faith

In the second place, Noah was saved because he believed God. As God puts it in Hebrews 11:7: *By faith Noah, being warned of God concerning things not seen as yet, moved with godly fear, prepared an ark to the saving of his house.* God told Noah that there was to be a flood, and Noah believed Him. Noah believed that there was to be a flood just because God said so. He had no other reason whatever for believing it; he asked for no other reason for believing it.

The wisest philosopher on earth is the man who has sense enough to believe what an infinitely wise God, who cannot lie, says, even if he has no other ground for believing it. And there is no bigger fool on earth than the would-be philosopher who doubts anything God says simply because he has no other ground for believing it than God's unsupported Word. The wisest man of his day said, *Seest thou a man wise in his own conceit? there is more hope of a fool than of him* (Proverbs 26:12). The puny, self-styled "philosophers" and would-be "scientists" of our day who are so *wise in [their] own conceit* that they venture to doubt God's Word because it does not agree with some of their educated notions would do well to lay this wise utterance of Solomon's to heart.

The Lord said, "There is to be a flood," and Noah had sense enough to believe it with all his heart – just because God said so. Thus *he condemned the world, and became heir of the righteousness which is according to faith* (Hebrews 11:7). And by his wise action in this matter, he not only *condemned the world* that existed then, but he also condemned a very large share of the world that now is. Happy is the man today who has as good sense in this matter as Noah had so many centuries ago.

There was no sign of a flood. The sun rose and set year after year, just as it always had. The laws of nature moved in their uniform course. No man of science saw anything indicative of an approaching flood. But God said to Noah, "There is to be a flood," and Noah believed it. People tried to laugh him out of it. They pointed to the steady course of the seasons and the uniformity of nature; they pointed to the fact that all of the great scientists were against him, and the theologians and the scholarly critics were all against him. Indeed, all kinds of scholars were against him; in fact, he stood entirely alone. Nevertheless, Noah stuck to his faith in God's word. Many doubtless said, "Noah, you are mistaken in thinking it is God's word. It is not God's word. If it were God's word, our great men would believe it." Some doubtless said that there was no God anyway, and that all this belief in God and God's word was mere empty superstition.

But Noah believed God in the face of it all, and it was well for him that he did. Unquestionably believing God's word saved him and his whole family from utter destruction. You and I must be saved in exactly the same way if we are saved at all. We also have God's word. The proof that this Book is God's word is overwhelmingly conclusive, and God's word, as found in this Book, tells of another coming judgment. It tells us that in that judgment many will be eternally lost. God's word about that is not generally believed. Many men of science do not believe it, and today many theological professors do not believe it; and some preachers even ridicule the idea. Many scoff at the very idea of God having a word at all, and some even question whether there is a God.

But there is a God, and this Book is God's Word. That can be easily proven. And God's Word says that there is to be a judgment of all mankind (Acts 17:31), and God's word about that judgment, just like God's word about the flood, will be fulfilled to the letter.

Our salvation depends upon our holding fast to God's Word and believing it to the very letter, in spite of objections and sneers and erroneous arguments of men, even of scholarly men. Oh, happy is the man who has sense enough to learn from the unvarying history of the past and believes what God says in spite of the proud unbelief of men, no matter who they may be.

Noah Was Saved by Obedience

In the third place, Noah was saved because he obeyed God. *And the* LORD *said unto Noah, Come thou and all thy house into the ark* (Genesis 7:1), and Noah came and brought all his house with him just as God had bidden him to do (Genesis 7:5). Noah's faith was a real faith. Noah's faith was not a mere opinion of the head. That sort of faith will not save anyone. Noah's faith was a faith of the heart, a faith that acts upon what it believes, and obeys the God it believes in. That is the only kind of faith that saves anybody. God said, *Make thee an ark* (Genesis 6:14), and He told Noah exactly how to make it. Noah made the ark exactly according to God's specifications. He attempted no improvements of his own upon God's plans. He was wise enough to do exactly as God told him. The ark God commanded him to build was on a vast scale, and it must have seemed like a huge undertaking. Not only that, it must have also seemed like an absurd undertaking. And it was a very expensive undertaking. No doubt, Noah was ridiculed. No doubt, men tried to dissuade him. No doubt, some of his most judicious and trusted friends pointed out more profitable ways to invest his money and more pleasant ways to employ his time, but Noah went right on doing exactly what God told him to do.

It is probable that he put all that he had into that old ark. He had nothing to base his hopes on but God's word, but that was enough. It was well for him that he relied on it. It is always well to depend on God's word. Very likely, it cost Noah his entire fortune to build the ark, and when the last nail was driven, he had nothing left. But when he came out of the ark he owned the whole earth. It was all his. There were no rival claimants. His title was clear and indisputable. All the men who had laughed at him were dead. They had lost everything. Noah had gained everything. So will it be with you and me, if we obey God. The one who obeys God may lose everything for the time being, but he will gain everything for eternity, for he becomes an heir of God and a joint heir with Christ (Romans 8:17).

God told Noah to build the ark for his own salvation and the salvation of his house. What does God command us to do for our salvation and that of our house? Acts 16:31 answers the question: *Believe on the Lord Jesus Christ, and thou shalt be saved, and thy house.* God commands us to believe *on* Jesus Christ, not to believe *about* Him, but to believe *on* Him. In other words, we need to accept Him, to take Him, to take Him as our Savior, and to take Him as our Lord and Master. We must surrender absolutely to His will and confess Him as our Lord and Master before the world (John 1:12; Romans 10:9-10).

Do that and you shall have life, eternal life. You will be ridiculed if you do. No doubt about that. If some young men who read these words accept Christ, their companions will make fun of them tomorrow morning. If some businessman accepts and confesses Christ, some of his business friends will make fun of him. If some wives accept Jesus Christ now, their husbands will certainly ridicule them.

It may cost any of these persons a good deal. It may cost some of them their position. It may cost some of them all they have in the world, just as it cost Noah. But it will pay. In one sense, they will gain more than even Noah did, though he gained the whole earth. They will gain an *inheritance incorruptible, and undefiled, and that fadeth not away, reserved in heaven for you* (1 Peter 1:4). They will become heirs of God and joint heirs with Jesus Christ. They may have to suffer with Christ, but the old Book of God says, *If so be that we suffer with him, that we [shall] be also glorified with him* (Romans 8:16-17).

When Noah came out of the ark safe and found the whole earth his, I do not think he regretted the ridicule he had endured, nor the money he had expended. And when you who read my words stand before God and all things are yours for all eternity, you will not regret the ridicule you may have endured, nor the money you have expended because of your belief in Jesus Christ and your obedience to God. On the other hand, when those who had ridiculed Noah saw the flood rising, they wished they too had invested all in an ark and were safely housed inside. So in the judgment day that is surely coming on this old world, those who sneer at the Christian now and ridicule the Christian now will wish that they too had invested their all in Jesus Christ. There were no more skeptics when the flood had done its work, and there will be no more skeptics or agnostics or theosophists in the judgment day. There will be a good many of you gentlemen and ladies who will wish you never had been skeptics or agnostics or theosophists or Christian Scientists, falsely so-called. I tell you, the smart young man who has caught a few of the stock phrases and arguments of modern infidelity, and goes around laughing at preachers and Christians and those who invite him to the church and to Christ will wish in that day that he had possessed more sense and had not ridiculed them.

Noah Was Saved Because He Accepted God's Invitation

In the fourth place, Noah was saved because he accepted God's invitation. God had said, *Come thou and all thy house into the ark,* and Noah just came. It was not merely the invitation that saved Noah but also his own acceptance of the invitation. That is what will decide the matter with each one of us. We are all invited. God says, *Whosoever will, let him take the water of life freely* (Revelation 22:17). The Lord Jesus says, *Him that cometh to me I will in no wise cast out* (John 6: 37). Will you accept the invitation or will you decline it? It is just as true of many today as it was when our Lord said it when He was here upon earth: *Ye will not come to me, that ye might have life* (John 5:40), and that is the sole reason why they are lost; they won't accept the invitation.

> It was not merely the invitation that saved Noah but also his own acceptance of the invitation.

A friend of mine told me a story many years ago. I do not know where he heard it, and of course, I cannot vouch for its truth, but it exactly illustrates my point. He said that a certain rich Christian worker who wished to illustrate how men are saved by simply accepting the gospel invitation offered to pay the debts of everyone who came to his office for that purpose. Most men naturally regarded it as a hoax or a trick of some kind and did not go to his office. One man believed it, at least enough to try it. He went, and the rich worker paid every penny of his debts. That man was saved from his burden of debt by accepting the invitation. The invitation was for all, but only the one who accepted it received the salvation offered in it.

Noah accepted God's invitation to *come into the ark* and was saved, and every one of us who accepts God's invitation to come into Jesus Christ by accepting Him as our personal Savior, surrendering to Him as our Lord, and confessing Him as such before the world, will be saved. Everyone who does not accept God's invitation to come into Christ will be lost. It is up to every one of you to say for yourself whether you will be saved or whether you will be lost, whether you will spend eternity in heaven or whether you will spend eternity in hell.

You decide that by your decision as to whether you will accept God's invitation or decline God's invitation.

Noah accepted the invitation for his family as well as for himself. He took them in with him. The whole family was gathered in. The record reads: *And Noah went in, and his sons, and his wife, and his sons' wives with him, into the ark* (Genesis 7:7). It has been said that it speaks well for Noah that in the midst of such prevailing unbelief, his whole household had such faith in the old man that they all accompanied him into the ark. Perhaps it speaks even better for his consistency, integrity, and nobility of character that his daughters-in-law had as much confidence in him as his own sons.

> It speaks well for Noah that in prevailing unbelief, his household had such faith in the old man that they accompanied him into the ark.

It is certainly more than can be said of many professing Christian parents today, that every member of their household follows them in the acceptance of Christ. I think the Bible plainly indicates that when a man's family does not come along with him, it is somehow the parents' fault. There is some screw loose somewhere in his character or his conduct. He is worldly or unloving or not strictly truthful or unchristian somewhere. Or he may neglect persistent prayer or wise, spirit-filled personal effort. In any case, God is saying, *Come thou and all thy house into the ark;* and He says in Acts 16:31, *Believe on the Lord Jesus, and thou shalt be saved, thou and thy house.* I do not see how any Christian man or woman can rest while even one child is out of the ark. Suppose Noah had found Shem, Ham, or Japheth lacking; do you not think he would have made a strenuous effort to find him and bring him in?

In the first church of which I was pastor, there were two women who were members of the church. One of these women, a farmer's wife, had a large family of children, but she saw to it that every one of them was saved. Several of them became missionaries. At least three of them are missionaries at the present time. The other woman's children were unsaved. The woman who had brought her own children to Christ one by one went to the other woman in a time of deep religious interest and tried to stir her up to win her own children to Christ. But the woman replied, "Oh, I believe they will all be saved . . . sometime." But they were not. One of them at least is dead now and died outside of Christ.

Dr. George Pentecost once talked with a young man whose mother was a professing Christian. The young man sneered at Christianity and at Christians. Dr. Pentecost said to him, "Oh, you think then that Christians are weak in their minds, that they have a soft spot in their brains somewhere, or that they are hypocrites?"

The young man replied, "Well, I don't like to put it just that way, but that is about what I think."

"But," said Dr. Pentecost, "isn't your mother a Christian?"

"Yes."

"Is your mother weak-minded or is she a hypocrite?"

"You have no right to speak that way of my mother," the young man hotly replied.

"No, but you said that all Christians had a soft spot in their brains somewhere, and you say your mother is a Christian."

The young man blushed, hesitated, and then replied, "If my mother really is a Christian, why then has she never spoken to me about my soul?"

That is what some of your children are thinking of some of you professing Christians. Which one of your children are you willing to have lost? Oh, if you have an unsaved child, let God's invitation sink down to the very depths of your heart: *Come thou and all thy house into the ark.*

The Lord Shut Him In

One more thing. Let me call your attention to five wonderfully expressive words in the biblical account of the flood. They are found in Genesis 7:16: *And the* LORD *shut him in.* When God shut the door of that ark, Noah was safe. The torrential rains might fall from above; the earth might subside beneath; the waters of the sea might rush in upon the doomed land, but Noah was safe inside the ark built according to God's pattern. And so it is with us once we are in the ark built according to God's pattern, when we are in Christ by accepting Him with our whole heart. When we accept Christ fully as our Savior, surrender to Him unreservedly as our Lord, and gladly confess Him as such before the world, God shuts us in, and we are safe. There may be appalling storms; there may be fierce tempests; there may be an awful judgment day. We may be weak in ourselves, but we are safe. That awful great tribulation of which the Bible so often speaks and toward which things seem to be so rapidly moving today, in Russia and Germany and England and even in America, may come, but we are safe, *shut in* the ark. And our Lord Jesus Himself says in John 10:28-29, *I give unto them eternal life; and they shall never perish, and no one shall snatch them out of my hand. My Father, which hath given them unto me, is greater than all; and no one is able to snatch them out of the Father's hand.*

It was not any strength or goodness of his own that made Noah safe in that awful day; it was being in the ark that made him safe. It is not any strength or goodness that you or I may have that makes us safe; it is being in Christ Jesus, being in the ark made on God's pattern, thoroughly well built. That ark will stand any storm.

But the door that shut Noah and his family in also shut the unbelieving world out, and when the door was once shut, the day of grace was ended. The door had stood open many years:

The longsuffering of God waited in the days of Noah, while the ark was a preparing (1 Peter 3:20). God's long-suffering grace had waited one hundred years and more. But the day of grace was over.

The day of grace will soon be over with you. The door is still open. It will be shut someday. It will be shut for some of you before another year passes; it will be shut for some of you before another month passes; it will be shut for some of you before another week passes; it will be shut for some of you before another day passes. Of course, I do not know who the people are who will read this solemn declaration. But whoever you are, do not presume on God's long-suffering mercy. Note the solemn words of Him who proved His love by dying to save you: *When once the master of the house is risen up, and hath shut to the door, and ye begin to stand without, and to knock at the door, saying, Lord, Lord, open to us; and he shall answer and say to you, I know you not whence ye are* (Luke 13:25).

> Do not presume on God's long-suffering mercy.

Let's think back to the last day of the antediluvian world. One of the most wonderful paintings I ever saw is Schorn's picture of the deluge in the new Alte Pinakothek in Munich, Germany. The painting is unfinished, but it is a masterpiece.

That day broke bright and clear as other days had. There was little sign of any approaching catastrophe. Noah had gone into the ark; the animals had gathered from near and far and gone in too, and the people had been a little startled by this strange procession of animals coming from the four points of the compass. But seven days had gone by since then and nothing had happened, and their fright had passed away (Genesis 7:4-10).

These seven days were seven days of deposed mercy. Not only had their fear passed away, so also had their opportunity. Men and women went about their ordinary pursuits again: *They were eating and drinking, marrying and giving in marriage, until the [very] day that Noah entered into the ark* (Matthew 24:38). Evening came on; the streets were crowded with people. In many a house, there were gay festal scenes. The sun went down in a cloud. There were rumblings of distant thunder. Men laugh and say, "This is a striking coincidence. Old Noah said the flood would come today, and really it does look like rain." The more-timid are fearful. The rain begins to patter in the streets, and people hurry on to their destination. Now the storm bursts in its fury. The heavens are illumined with white and purple light; then all is dark. The thunder roars and reverberates; the water falls in cloudbursts; the earth seems to be sinking. It *is* sinking. It is slowly sinking beneath the level of the sea. The waters of the lake overflow, and the Caspian Sea will soon burst its ancient barriers and flood the entire inhabited earth. Yes, the waters are pouring in now, *the fountains of the great deep [are] broken up.* Terror-stricken men and women with ashen faces flee from theaters, ballrooms, and homes to the hills and to the mountains! Still, the land is sinking, and the waters are rising. The beasts of prey forget their savage instincts and cower beside terror-stricken men and women. Higher and higher rise the waters. Strong men fight with feeble women for the place of vantage. The waters sweep over a low hill, and a hundred souls huddled upon it are swept into eternity.

Look! On yonder hill stand a husband and wife alone. The waters are fast coming nearer and nearer. With her former love turned into savage hate, the woman turns on the man she has loved and cries, "Man, you have deceived me, ruined me. I longed to enter the ark and you laughed me out of it." The remorseless waters sweep them away together.

Look again! There is a maiden. She also had longed to enter the ark, but none of her friends had gone in, and she was unwilling to go alone. The waters sweep her away on their angry bosom, and soon the fair face sinks beneath the flood. Farther out is a man who had mocked Noah's faith, but now fear and agony are depicted on his distorted countenance; then it sinks beneath the flood. A young man who has pondered long in indecision turns an appealing look toward heaven, but it is too late, and he too sinks beneath the engulfing waters. Thus they go down, singly, by pairs, by hundreds, until the last man of the unbelieving world has disappeared. The end has come. The whole land is submerged, not an unbeliever left; but in the distance floats the ark of God in safety, while the moon sheds its gentle light upon the unbroken surface of the great deep.

There is another day of doom fast approaching. God tells us in this Book: *He hath appointed a day, in the which he will judge the world in righteousness by that man whom he hath ordained; whereof he hath given assurance unto all men, in that he hath raised him from the dead* (Acts 17:31).

Are you ready for that day? Come into the ark. Believe God. Obey God. Accept the invitation; accept Jesus Christ. Confess Him before the world. Let the world laugh if it will. Some of you in the deepest impulses of your heart would like to get right down on your knees now and beg God for mercy. Do it. Don't mind what people say. Don't mind who laughs. Come into the ark.

Chapter 9

Time and Eternity Contrasted

For our light affliction, which is but for a moment, worketh for us a far more exceeding and eternal weight of glory; while we look not at the things which are seen, but at the things which are not seen: for the things which are seen are [for a season]; but the things which are not seen are [for eternity] (2 Corinthians 4:17-18).

The apostle Paul had to endure some things that to most men would seem very hard to bear, and some of these afflictions continued through many years. Indeed, the thirty years of his Christian experience seem, at first sight, like thirty years of self-denial and suffering for Christ. But in speaking of these afflictions in our text, Paul speaks of them as *our light affliction* and also as our affliction *which is but for a moment.*

Is thirty years "but a moment"? Yes, when compared with eternity. Your life of eighty or ninety years or one hundred years is but the twinkling of an eye when compared with eternity. And is the loss of friends, the loss of ease, the loss of the admiration and applause of men, the loss of home and native land, the loss of all that men ordinarily hold dear a *light affliction*? And is imprisonment, shipwreck, scourging, wandering, hunger, and stoning considered *light afflictions*? Yes they are, when compared with the joy and honor and glory which are to be revealed in us in a glad day that is soon coming.

When the sufferings of this present time are put in comparison with the eternal glories that are secured, they are nothing at all. And when all the wealth and pleasure and honors that one can possibly get in this world are compared to the eternal agony, ruin, despair, and shame that it costs to live for this world, they too are nothing.

Suppose one gets a million dollars, two million dollars, or one hundred million dollars at the cost of being lost forever. Is it worth it? Suppose one's whole life from boyhood or girlhood to old age is one constant round of parties, feasts, frolics, and merriments at the cost of spending an eternity in hell. Is it worth it? The truly wise man does not look at the things which are seen, which are for a time, but at the things which are unseen, which are for eternity. This, then, is really our subject here: ETERNITY.

There Is an Eternity and We Must Go There

The first thing our text teaches us and which we know to be true is that there is an eternity, and we must go there. It is the height of folly to refuse to think about eternity.

A lady said to me one day, speaking of a certain shiftless young man who had had great opportunities in life but had thrown them all away, "He just lives for today; he never thinks of the future either in the life that now is or the life that is to come." Everybody sees that the young man is an idiot. I do not think there is any difference of opinion on that point among any of those who know him. But is he really much more of a blockhead than the man or the woman who lives only for the brief days that we spend on this earth and never thinks of that vast eternity which stretches beyond to which we are all hurrying at express speed? There is an eternity. I may live ninety or a hundred years of the life that now is, but I shall certainly live millions and billions and trillions of years in the endless eons of years in the life that is to come. I shall live forever and forever.

Eternity is the important thing. The life we now have is important only because it determines our eternity. Many a man who is wise enough to look somewhat into the future asks himself the question, "Where and how shall I spend my middle life, and where and how shall I spend my old age?" A man who is still wiser will ask himself the question, "Where and how shall I spend my eternity?" Have you settled that question? Let me put it to every one of my readers: Have you settled where and how you will spend eternity? If you have not, there is only one sane thing for you to do, and that is to settle the question now as to where and how you will spend eternity.

Where and How of Our Eternity

The second thing that I wish to address is that where and how we shall spend eternity is settled in this life. The life that we live now is the preparation time, and it is the only preparation time for the life that is to come. Time is the preparation time and the only preparation time for eternity.

The boy who has wasted his school days and failed to prepare for business life would gladly go back and live his wasted boyhood over again when he gets into the weary grind of a life that is the inevitable outcome of a wasted boyhood and young manhood, but he cannot. Much less can any man or woman who wastes this present life on earth come back from a ruined eternity and live this present life over. It cannot be done. You are making your eternity today.

Men have tried to believe that there is some other time to prepare for the future for those who waste this present opportunity in this life. Such a hope is the baseless fabric of a dream, which has not one atom of foundation either in common sense or in the more sure Word of God. "If," says Jesus, "you *die in your sins: whither I go, ye cannot come*" (John 8:21). This word of our Lord Himself makes it as clear as day that where and how we shall spend eternity is settled in this life; it is settled on this side of the grave.

You are making your eternity now. Some young man or woman may be saying in their heart, "I will go out and have one more fling at sin." Do it, and it may land you in hell for all eternity. In the lost world of endless midnight and despair, you will look up and say, "Dr. Torrey told me that if I went out to spend one more night in sin, I would spend eternity in hell, and here I am." And you will wring your hands, and you will shriek, and you will agonize, and you will despair, but it will be too late, too late forever.

I was dealing one night with a man in Minneapolis who was under deep conviction of sin. I urged him to immediately accept Jesus Christ, but he hesitated and left without deciding. He thought he would go into a saloon and have one more drink, and he did, and that led to another, and so on. Two years later I received a letter from him from the state prison at Stillwater, telling me how near he had come to accepting Christ that night, but how he had gone to have another drink and then another. He told of how he had become intoxicated, and while intoxicated he had stolen an overcoat; he was arrested, tried, and found guilty. He had no recollection of stealing the coat but said he had no doubt that he did. He was sentenced to two years in Stillwater State Prison. He added, "I have accepted Christ here, but these two years have been wasted because I did not do as you urged me to that night." But ah, that is not so bad as to wake up in hell and know that you are to spend all eternity there because you did not take the step that you know you ought to take now.

How to Secure a Blessed and Glorious Eternity

We have seen that there is an eternity; we have seen that where and how we shall spend eternity is settled in the life that we live now. So we come face to face with the question, What must I do in the life that I have now that I may have a satisfactory and glorious eternity?

First of all, if you are to have a satisfactory and glorious eternity, you must believe on Jesus Christ in your life now. God tells us this in His Word over and over again. For example, He says in John 3:36, *He that believeth on the Son hath everlasting life: and he that believeth not the Son shall not see life; but the wrath of God abideth on him.*

And He says in Romans 6:23, *The wages of sin is death; but the gift of God is eternal life through Jesus Christ our Lord.* The first thing to do, then, if we are to have a satisfactory and glorious eternity, the first thing we must do if we are to spend eternity outside of hell is to believe on the Lord Jesus Christ.

Just what does it mean to believe on the Lord Jesus Christ? God Himself answers that question in John 1:12: *As many as received him, to them gave he power to become the sons of God, even to them that believe on his name.* Here we are told that to believe on Jesus Christ, to *believe on his name*, is to *receive him*. That is to simply accept Him to be to us what God offers Him to be to everyone – the Savior who has borne our sins for us, borne them in His own body on the cross, and is therefore ready and able to forgive all our sins as soon as we confess them and forsake them. We must put our trust in Him, to receive Him also as our Lord and Master to whom we surrender the entire control of our lives, and receive Him as our divine teacher to whom we surrender our thoughts. Whatever else we may or may not do, it is certain we shall not have a blessed eternity if we do not receive Jesus Christ.

In the second place, if we are to have a satisfactory and glorious eternity, we must serve Jesus Christ. We are saved by grace, but we are rewarded according to our works.

Eternity begins with the coming of Christ, and at His coming, Jesus Christ *shall reward every man according to his works* (Matthew 16:27). Our eternity will be rich and full in proportion to the faithfulness of our service here on earth. There are many who think that all professing Christians will have an equally glorious eternity, but this is pure delusion. It contradicts the plain teachings of the Word of God and the teachings of sanctified common sense as well. The Word of God tells us that some will be saved *so as by fire* (1 Corinthians 3:15), but others will have an abundant entrance *into the everlasting kingdom of our Lord and Saviour Jesus Christ* (2 Peter 1:11). The one who barely accepts Christ, who holds on to the world in a measure, and who does scarcely anything for his Master will have no such entrance into *the everlasting kingdom of our Lord and Saviour Jesus Christ.* He will have no such glorious eternity as the one who turns away from the world with his whole heart and gives up all its follies and self-indulgences and comes out and is separate and lives wholly for Christ, a life of constant self-denial and constant service.

Professing Christians, do you realize that you are preparing your eternity by the way you serve Christ in your life today? Do you realize that your eternity will be richer or poorer by the way in which you serve Jesus Christ on earth? Do you realize that every day you spend in hard service will make heaven that much richer, and every day and hour frittered away will make heaven that much poorer? Ponder again those familiar words that God spoke to Daniel: *They that be wise shall shine as the brightness of the firmament; and they that turn many to righteousness as the stars for ever and ever* (Daniel 12:3). How important then is every day of our Christian life. Let me ask you the question, Has today counted as much as it might have counted for eternity?

Again, let me say that the sufferings we endure, and the sacrifices we make for Christ will make eternity richer. The words of our Lord Jesus are very plain on this point; He says, *Blessed are ye when men shall reproach you, and persecute you, and say all manner of evil against you falsely, for my sake. Rejoice, and be exceeding glad: for great is your reward in heaven: for so persecuted they the prophets which were before you* (Matthew 5:11-12).

There are some who bitterly regret it when they are called upon to be reproached or slandered or in any way to suffer persecution for Jesus Christ's sake. Far from regretting it, we should rejoice in it instead; we should be *exceeding glad,* because these things bring great reward in heaven. Every sneer that one endures, every reproach that is heaped upon us, every loss that we sustain for the sake of the truth and for the sake of the Lord Jesus Christ brings glorious reward in eternity.

Never forget what Paul said: *For I reckon that the sufferings of this present time are not worthy to be compared with the glory which shall be revealed to us-ward* (Romans 8:18), and how he says, *If [I] suffer, [I] shall also reign with him* (2 Timothy 2:12). The seemingly awful tortures endured by the Armenian Christians rather than give up their faith in Christ, which to some people seem so incomprehensible, are no longer a mystery if we bear in mind how they will bring reward a thousandfold throughout all eternity. Don't whine, but thank God every time it is your privilege to suffer for Christ; the more you suffer the more you can rejoice. The opportunity to suffer for Christ or for the truth is an opportunity for an investment that pays an eternal dividend.

Also, if we would have a thoroughly satisfactory and glorious eternity, we must use our money for Jesus Christ. The use we make of our money in this life enriches or impoverishes our eternity. The apostle Paul says in 1 Timothy 6:17-19, *Charge them that are rich in this present world, that they be not highminded, nor have their hope set on the uncertainty of riches, but on God, who giveth us richly all things to enjoy; that they do good, that they be rich in good works, that they be ready to distribute, willing to communicate; laying up in store for themselves a good foundation against the time to come, that they may lay hold on the life which is life indeed.*

And the Lord Jesus says in Matthew 6:19-20, *Lay not up for yourselves treasures upon the earth, where moth and rust doth consume, and where thieves break through and steal: but lay up for yourselves treasures in heaven, where neither moth nor rust doth consume, and where thieves do not break through nor steal.*

How few people seem to realize that they are making their eternity by their use of their money here on earth, but it is so. I think some of us will look back with regret from the other world and say, "What a fool I was to invest my money in houses and lands and jewels and luxuries, in novelties and trinkets, when I might have invested it so it would be paying me interest today."

Men and women, the greatest practical question that confronts you and me is where shall we spend eternity and how shall we spend eternity? Will you spend eternity in heaven or will you spend eternity in hell? Will you spend it in joy and glory unutterable, or will you spend it in misery and shame unutterable? Time is nothing compared to eternity. Ten, twenty, eighty years are nothing compared to eternity – eternity! That is the all-important matter. Where you will spend eternity and how you will spend eternity will be determined by your action in this life; it will be in a measure determined by your action today. What you do today is of tremendous importance. If you have not already accepted Christ, accept Him now. And even if you have accepted Christ but have been serving Him in a halfhearted way, give yourself up wholly to Him from this time forward. If you have been holding back from sacrificing for Christ, make the sacrifice at once. I desire with all my heart that my eternity be just as rich, just as full, just as glorious as possible, and by God's grace I am going to make it so, whatever it costs.

> Give yourself up wholly to Him.

Chapter 10

Eternal Life or the Wrath of God: Which Will You Choose?

He that believeth on the Son hath everlasting life: and he that believeth not the Son shall not see life; but the wrath of God abideth on him. (John 3:36)

We have in these words of God a most vivid contrast. I know of no verse in the Bible that is more full of glory in the first part and more full of darkest despair in the last part. It presents God's alternatives, alternatives open to all: eternal life for all those who believe on the Son, and the wrath of God for those who refuse to believe on Him. It leaves each one of us to choose which we shall have.

One of the most meaningful and glorious phrases that was ever uttered is that which was so often on the lips of our Lord Jesus Christ: *eternal life*. One of the most awful and appalling phrases ever uttered is that other phrase which occurs in our text: *the wrath of God*. We cannot put into words or even conceive in our imagination the wealth of glory there is wrapped up in those two words, *eternal life,* nor can we put into words or conceive by human imagination the depth of dishonor, horror, shame, woe, and despair that is wrapped up in that other phrase, *the wrath of God*. It is between these two, the unutterably glorious eternal life and the immeasurably and unspeakably awful wrath of God, that each of us is called to make his choice: *He that believeth on the Son hath everlasting life: and he that believeth not the Son shall not see life; but the wrath of God abideth on him.*

The question, then, that confronts each of us in this place is this: Eternal life or the wrath of God? Which shall it be? Which shall I choose? That should not be a difficult question to settle. If any man is not a hopeless fool or an utter maniac, he will certainly say, "Give me eternal life; as for the wrath of God, Jesus, Thou Son of God, save me from that." But that is not the choice that some of you really are making today. You are deliberately turning your backs on eternal life, and you have been turning your backs on eternal life for years. Some of you are deliberately choosing the wrath of God, and you have been choosing the wrath of God for years.

How can we doubt the existence of a personal devil of great cunning and great power when we see how men are so utterly blinded and deceived by his cunning, and so completely enslaved mentally by his power that they choose the wrath of God rather than eternal life? The existence of such a devil as the Bible presents is the only rational explanation for this indisputable fact. You question the existence of a personal devil, yet you yourselves are living demonstrations of his existence and of his marvelous cunning and his exceedingly great power.

The Things Contrasted

Now let's look more closely at the two possibilities that are put in such vivid contrast. We cannot possibly conceive of the glory of the one or the horror of the other, but we can get some hint of what they mean.

Eternal Life – What Is It?

In the first place, *eternal life is real life*. In 1 Timothy 6:19 Paul says, *Lay hold on eternal life*. The Revised Version translates this differently. It reads: *Lay hold on the life which is life indeed*. The Revised Version gives the correct translation, and that is what eternal life is – *life Indeed,* life not merely in seeming but life also in reality. Much that we call life is not really life at all, but death.

Many a young man or woman plunges into a life of gaiety, worldliness, and sin, and cries as they do it, "I am going to see life for myself." No, you are not going to see life; you are going to see death. Paul was right when he said, *She that liveth in pleasure is dead while she liveth* (1 Timothy 5:6). It is really God who says it, God speaking through Paul. Life is not what you see in the saloon with its revelry; that is death. Life is not what you see in the gambling house with its strange fascination and intense excitement; that is death. Life is not what you see in the theater with its appeal to your lust and your impure fantasy, with its many-times-married actresses with their fair faces and foul hearts and with its actors who are so often the wreckers of happy homes; that is death. Life is not what you see in the movies with their constant appeal to all that is vulgar and vile in men and women; that is death. Life is not what you see in the ballroom where supposedly decent women permit a familiarity of approach and contact that is nowhere else permitted except by the most indecent women; that is death. Life is not what you see in the costly receptions of the rich with their vain display of jewels, fine apparel, and disgusting and shocking immodesty in dress; that is death.

Anywhere and everywhere, a life of sin is death; a life of selfishness is death; a life of pleasure is death (1 Timothy 5:6); a life of worldliness is death. These are not life, they are death. But *eternal life* really is life; it is *life indeed*. It deserves the name *life,* and no one really knows what life is who has not received eternal life through Jesus Christ our Lord. Eternal life is life indeed.

In the second place, *eternal life is fullness of life.* It is life abundant. Jesus once said, *I came that they may have life, and may have it abundantly* (John 10:10). Eternal life is life full of beauty, full of peace, full of joy, full of power, full of glory, abundant life, abounding life, overflowing life.

In the third place, *eternal life is satisfying life.* No life but eternal life can ever satisfy the longing and capacity of these souls of ours made in the likeness of God. No life that is purely earthly; no life that we inherit from our ancestors, no matter how fine they may have been and how refined in character, can satisfy our souls. No life but the life we derive directly from God when we receive the Lord Jesus Christ, no life but eternal life can satisfy the infinite yearnings of these spirits of ours made originally in the image of God. Even in the most depraved of us, our infinite longings retain traces of that divine image in which we were made.

"Give me wealth," one man cries, "and I shall be satisfied."

"Give me power," another cries, "and I shall be satisfied."

"Give me pleasure," another cries, "and I shall be satisfied."

"Give me fame," another cries, "and I shall be satisfied."

No, you will not be satisfied with any of these or with all of these. You would be better off to cry, "Give me God, and I shall be satisfied; give me eternal life, and I shall be satisfied." Oh, how many I have known to whom this world seemed to have given all that it had to give, but they were not satisfied. And how many I have known to whom this world had given very little of all it has to give, and yet they were satisfied, for they had God, and they had eternal life.

In the fourth place, *eternal life is life of highest knowledge.* Our Lord brings that out in a wonderful way in an utterance that He made at one of the supreme moments of His life. In His prayer with His disciples the night before His crucifixion, as He lifted His eyes to heaven and spoke to the Father, He said, *This is life eternal, that they should know thee the only true God, and him whom thou didst send, even Jesus Christ* (John 17:3). Eternal life is full knowledge of the infinite One. The knowledge that the most educated scholar has gathered from books, the knowledge that the most intellectual philosopher has deduced for himself, or the knowledge that the most brilliant scientist has discovered as he studied the rocks beneath his feet or the stars above his head is nothing compared to the knowledge that the humblest man or woman obtains who enters into eternal life. They receive knowledge of God, full knowledge of the infinite One.

In the fifth place, *eternal life is perfect life, completeness of life.* It is life in its perfection, in its completeness. All other life than the eternal life, which we receive when we receive Jesus Christ, is partial, fragmentary, unbalanced, and incomplete. *Eternal life* is life perfected, filled out, perfectly balanced, and complete. We have a suggestion of this in the words of Paul to Timothy where he says, *From a babe thou hast known the sacred writings which are able to make thee wise unto salvation through faith which is in Christ Jesus. Every scripture inspired of God is also profitable for teaching, for reproof, for correction, for instruction which is in righteousness: that the man of God may be complete, furnished completely unto every good work* (2 Timothy 3:15-17).

Here we see that a saving knowledge of Jesus Christ comes through the written Word, and thus eternal life comes through the Word, as John puts it: *These are written, that ye might believe that Jesus is the Christ, the Son of God; and that believing ye might have life through his name* (John 20:31). And we further see that by receiving eternal life through the Word, a man becomes *complete;* he obtains complete life, eternal life.

In the sixth place, *eternal life is divine life, the very life of God imparted to us.* The apostle John says in his first epistle, *And the life was manifested* [that is, manifested in the person of Jesus Christ], *and we have seen, and bear witness, and declare unto you the life, the eternal life, which was with the Father, and was manifested unto us* (1 John 1:2). Eternal life, then, is the life of the infinitely Holy and blessed God, the infinite life imparted to us. Oh, it is wonderful and amazing! Think of it; this is your privilege and my privilege. My privilege, a poor sinner, an ignoramus, a worm of the dust, one whose heart was once set upon the silly follies of the world and revolting sin, is to have the life of the blessed God, the very life of God Himself, this infinite life, imparted to me!

In the seventh place, *eternal life is endless life.* Endlessness is not the most essential characteristic of eternal life, for its quality is more important than its duration, but nevertheless it is endless. I thank God it is. I thank God that He offers me a life that is not only infinite in its quality but also endless in its duration. I cannot be satisfied with anything that ever comes to an end. I love flowers. I look with joy upon the little daisy in the grass, the pansy with its happy, sweetly speaking face, the lily of the valley in its modesty and purity and matchless beauty. I look upon the rose in its rich, superb splendor, the dearest of all flowers to me; but as I look upon an exquisite bunch of roses, sadness steals over me, for I cannot help but think of how soon they will fade. "Leaf by leaf, the roses fall; drop by drop, the springs run dry."[6]

I love nature, especially the glorious beauty of a sunset in the mountains or by the sea. But as I look at the green and the crimson, the azure and the gold, and it seems as if the very gates of heaven were about to swing open, it all fades. Night descends and I am chilled and lonely. I love high and noble and ennobling human friendships in which I have been peculiarly favored of God; but a few years pass, and they are broken by separation or by death, and it is all over. Nothing but a memory and a heartache remain.

So it is with everything on earth; it ends. Thank God for something that never ends, something that always has the freshness of the dawn in it, something that stretches on and on and on into the boundless spaces of ever-increasing glory before you. Thank God for *everlasting life*. Such is eternal life, real life, fullness of life, satisfying life, life of highest knowledge, complete life, the life of God imparted to us, and life that never ends.

> So it is with everything on earth; it ends. Thank God for something that never ends.

Don't you desire it? Don't you desire it with an intensity that will not take no for an answer? I do. I would sacrifice everything I hold dear on earth to obtain it. I would still think I had made a good bargain even if it should cost me everything that men hold dear on earth. Thank God, eternal life is mine! It is mine! It is mine! I have it now. I already have it in its beginnings, and I have the sure promise of its fullness. I shall never lose it (John 10:28-29). Will you have it too?

The wrath of God. What is that?

It is just what the words express. I have given a good deal of

---

6   Caroline Dana Howe, "Leaf by Leaf the Roses Fall," 1856.

study to the etymology and the usage of the Greek word which is rendered *wrath* in this verse. It means "the intense and settled displeasure of God," "the intense displeasure of that infinitely Holy Being who created us and all things and has the absolute control of all the powers and forces of the universe."

Every true and wise husband dreads the displeasure of his wife; that is, if it could be avoided, he would not do anything to incur her displeasure. Every true and wise citizen dreads the displeasure of his government. Every true son dreads the displeasure of his father. But how much more will every man of understanding and of character dread the wrath of God. The wrath of God! There is nothing more awful than that. To have the infinitely Holy One displeased with you, to have the Holy Being, before whom the seraphim veil their faces and cry, "Holy, Holy, Holy, is the Lord God Almighty," displeased with you, and to have the omnipotent and infinite ruler of the universe displeased with you is a fearful thing. To have the mighty One who holds the sun, moon, stars, and all the myriad systems of worlds of light that stud the endless expanse of heaven in the hollow of His hand, as they move through space with incredible momentum displeased with you is a terrible thing. To have the infinitely wise ruler and shaper of the whole history of this tiny ball that we call the earth displeased with you, and yes, to have God displeased with you, to incur His wrath, His intense, deep-seated, settled displeasure – that is awful! That is horrifying! But that is certainly what stares in the face of many a man and many a woman here. *The wrath of God.* Gather your thoughts together. Think of it! Will you have it? Will you choose it?

Here then are before you the two alternatives. On the one hand is eternal life, real life, fullness of life, satisfying life, life of highest knowledge, complete life, the life of God, never-ending life, blessedness and glory, *eternal life.* On the other hand is the wrath of God, the intense, deep-seated, settled displeasure of the all-Holy One, the Maker and Governor of the universe. Which will you choose? If you choose the latter, some day you will be among those who *say to the mountains and to the rocks, Fall on us, and hide us from the face of him that sitteth on the throne, and from the wrath of the Lamb: for the great day of their wrath is come; and who is able to stand?* (Revelation 6:16-17).

Eternal Life or the Wrath of God

Now we come to the question, and it is a tremendously important question, By what act do we determine whether eternal life or the wrath of God is to be our portion? Note God's own answer to this immensely important question. It is not the answer of all modern philosophers; it is not the answer of all modern theologians; it is not the answer of all modern preachers, but it is God's answer, and therefore it is true. That answer is in the words of our text: *He that believeth on the Son hath everlasting life: and he that believeth not the Son shall not see life; but the wrath of God abideth on him.* Nothing could be more plain, simple, or unmistakable than this answer. The one and only act by which we get eternal life is the act of believing on the Son of God, believing on Jesus Christ. The one and only act by which we lose eternal life and bring upon ourselves the abiding wrath of God is by refusing to believe on Jesus Christ.

Whosoever believeth on Jesus Christ gets eternal life. There it stands in God's sure Word in language a child can understand: *He that believeth on the Son hath everlasting life,* regardless of who he is or what he is and regardless of what he has been or what he has done. He may be a millionaire or he may be a pauper; he may be a scholar or he may be unable to read or write; he may be moral, upright, and clean, or he may be immoral and dishonest and vile. But the moment any man, woman, or child believes on the Son, believes on Jesus Christ, that person gets eternal life. They get the actual experience of the beginnings of that life, and the fullness that awaits them in the world to come is assured. Any man or woman may get eternal life right now. You may get eternal life before you read another page in this book if you desire to do so, and you can have that perfect assurance that comes from knowing that you have God's own Word for your guarantee.

But what does it mean to believe on the Son of God? It is to accept God's testimony about Jesus Christ, that Jesus is the Christ, the Son of God; it is to act on that testimony by putting your full and absolute confidence in Him who is so entirely worthy of your confidence. It is to accept Him to be all that He offers Himself to be – your crucified Savior who bore every one of your sins in His own body on the cross and thus settled them. It is to accept your risen Savior who has all power in heaven and on earth and is able to keep you day by day. It is to take Him as your absolute Lord and Master to whom you surrender the entire control of your thoughts and life. Believing on the Lord Jesus Christ is putting your confidence in Him. It leads you to entrust to Him your salvation and to entrust to Him your whole self.

> Believing on the Lord Jesus Christ is putting your confidence in Him.

Believing on the Son of God will lead you to go right to Jesus Christ, the Son of God, and say to Him, "Lord Jesus, I believe God's testimony about you – that you are God's Son, that you bore my sins in your own body on the cross, and that you rose again and are a living Savior today. I commit myself to you to save and keep and guide and teach and govern me, to do what you will with me. I put my trust in you to save me from the guilt of sin by your atoning death. I put my trust in you to save me from the power of sin day by day by your resurrection power; I surrender to you the entire control of my life and thoughts."

It is this unreserved commitment of yourself to Jesus Christ that brings eternal life, and when you make it, you can say with Paul, *I know whom I have believed, and am persuaded that he is able to keep that which I have committed unto him against that day* (2 Timothy 1:12).

Will you take that decisive step? You have every reason for believing on the Son of God. The testimony that He really is the Son of God, God's own testimony to that fact, is unanswerable. Will you yield to the testimony and believe on Him?

Now what is the act by which we bring upon ourselves the wrath of God? Oh, the answer to that is so plain. Here it is: *He that believeth not the Son shall not see life; but the wrath of God abideth on him.* The Revised Version renders it: *He that obeyeth not the Son shall not see life, but the wrath of God abideth on him.* The truth is in both the Authorized and the Revised Versions, but neither the Authorized nor the Revised gives the exact force of the word which is translated *believeth not* in the one case and *obeyeth not* in the other. The word so translated means "to refuse to be persuaded; to refuse to believe," so exactly translated it would be "but he that refuseth to believe (or disbelieveth) the Son shall not see life, but the wrath of God abideth on him." The thought is that those who have heard of Him and do not believe are responsible for not believing, for they have refused to be persuaded by the evidence. They have refused to yield to the evidence; they have refused to believe. That is the exact truth about everyone who goes without believing on the Son of God, without putting their confidence in the Son of God, and without accepting the Son of God as their Savior, their Lord, their King.

You have had abundant evidence that He is the Son of God. You have had abundant evidence that He can save from the guilt and power of sin, but due to love of the world, love of sin, fear of man, or some other reason, you have refused to believe; you have not believed on the Son. Well, if you do not believe on the

Son of God, Jesus Christ our Lord, if you continue to refuse to yield to the evidence that Jesus is the Christ, the Son of God, with that real faith that leads to obedience to His Word and trust in Him, then you will not get eternal life. No, not only that, but you will also get the wrath of God.

Do you believe Jesus Christ? Do you believe Him with that real faith that leads you to act upon what He says, with that faith that leads you to put your unhesitating confidence in His promises and yield unquestioning obedience to His commands and put your confidence in Him? If not, *the wrath of God abideth on* you. It makes absolutely no difference who or what you are. You may not be a criminal or a moral monster; you may not be crude, selfish, and dishonest. You may not be contemptible and mean; you may be refined, sophisticated, and highly cultured. You may be a university student or a university professor; you may be amiable, gentlemanly, or ladylike; you may be true, kind, and generous. But if you do not believe on the Son of God, and refuse to be persuaded by His words to put confidence in Him as your atoning Savior, your risen Savior, and are not ready to act upon His every word, then the wrath of God abideth on you. The deep, settled, intense wrath of God is resting upon every man and woman, young and old, who does not put confidence in Jesus Christ as the Christ, the Son of God, and who does not stand ready to act upon His every word. *He that believeth not the Son shall not see life; but the wrath of God abideth on him.* Oh, it is awful! Awful! Awful!

If we could represent God's wrath by a black thundercloud and see things as they really are, we would see a blacker storm cloud than human eyes ever beheld hanging over the head of many a man and many a woman today, ready to break. I have been an eyewitness of some terrific storms on sea and land. I was once in a house that was struck by lightning, and at another time, I was standing in the doorway of another house when the lightning struck and splintered a great oak a few feet away. A part of the lightning passed through the very door where I was standing. One summer at Northfield, I had to go out into an electrical storm to quiet a horse that was trembling like a leaf and take him from underneath a tree. In a short time the lightning struck three times within sight of where I stood.

But I had a dream one night far more terrible than anything I ever saw in life. It was more than twenty years ago, but I remember it vividly, and recall the appalling horror that swept over me in the midst of the dream even now. Enormous bags of black, smoke-like, cyclonic clouds with ragged edges rolled up full of wind and electricity, and every moment I expected to see one burst and shoot down awful death upon my poor devoted head with deafening reverberation. I believe that awful dream that made my blood fairly run cold even in my sleep is only a faint picture of every man and woman today who is without Christ. The wrath of God abideth on you. That awful storm cloud, full of lightning, thunder, death, shame, woe, and despair, hangs over your head now, ready to burst.

But God is long-suffering and merciful; He is *not willing that any should perish* (2 Peter 3:9) and holds back the execution of His long pent-up wrath. Even more, He offers you eternal life – real life, fullness of life, perfectly satisfying life, life of highest knowledge, complete life, His own life, endless life, infinite life, life of measureless joy and beauty and power and glory. Which will you have? Eternal life or the wrath of God? Do I hear someone mutter, "I do not like that kind of preaching. I do not believe it." Then you are giving the lie to God, for it is not I but God who says, *He that believeth on the Son hath everlasting life: and he that believeth not the Son shall not see life; but the wrath of God abideth on him.* Oh, men and women, there are two possibilities open before you today: one infinitely glorious, the other inconceivably appalling. Eternal life or the wrath of God, which will you take?

Chapter 11

A Perfect Cure for Poverty and All Other Evils of the Day

Come unto me, all ye that labour and are heavy laden, and I will give you rest. Take my yoke upon you, and learn of me; for I am meek and lowly in heart: and ye shall find rest unto your souls. For my yoke is easy, and my burden is light.
(Matthew 11:28-30)

Human life is full of evils: poverty, sickness, bereavement, failure, bitterness of heart, despair, and death. If we could see all the tears that have been shed in America today, hear all the sighs, groans, wails, and shrieks that have been uttered, or witness the heartbreak and despair that have found no visible or audible expression, we would believe in hell – not in a hell lying beyond the grave, but a hell existing right here and now. That might make it easier for us to believe in a hell hereafter.

But is there no cure? Must this all go on and on forever? No, it need not go on. There is a perfect cure for all the ills that man is heir to – a cure that is sovereign, sufficient, sure, and speedy.

Jesus Christ announced that cure nearly nineteen hundred years ago, but the overwhelming majority of men and women have not listened, so our evils, miseries, and despair continue. This cure that our Lord Jesus Christ proposed for all our ills is in Matthew 11:28-30: *Come unto me, all ye that labour and are heavy laden, and I will give you rest. Take my yoke upon you, and learn of me; for I am meek and lowly in heart: and ye shall find rest unto your souls. For my yoke is easy, and my burden is light.*

Christ Jesus Himself is the cure for all our evils. He came to *destroy the works of the devil* (1 John 3:8). He does it for all who receive Him. Poverty, sickness, bereavement, failure, bitterness of heart, despair, and death, as well as sin and unbelief are all works of the devil, and we can be done with them by coming to Jesus, the Christ of God.

I propose to take up these various evils and show how Jesus, the Christ of God, is the cure for them, and how each one of us may be done with them right now.

Jesus Christ Is the Cure for Sin

We begin with the greatest of all evils – sin. Men tell us poverty is an evil, and I believe it. They tell us sickness is an evil, and I believe that too. But the monster evil, the evil that lies at the root of all other evils, is sin. Sin is the first great evil to get rid of. The preachers of the social gospel and all these philanthropists who are trying to lift men out of their miseries while leaving them in their sins mean well, but they are attempting the impossible and admit utter disappointment. It is like trying to rid men of some sickness by attacking the symptoms and not going to the root of the disease itself. It is like trying to cure smallpox by merely painting the pustules. Sin is the radical evil, the root evil, so we begin there, and that is where we all need to begin in our own lives. Jesus Christ is the cure for sin.

Christ Jesus Is the Cure for Sin in the Individual
First of all, Christ Jesus saves from the guilt of sin. Sin cuts men off from God. God is infinitely holy, so sin makes a great gulf between us and the Holy Being who rules this universe, the Being whom we call God, the only Being who is worthy to be called God. Separated from God, cast off from His grace and power, it is impossible for us to fight sin in our own strength. But Jesus Christ removes the barrier between God and us. He takes our guilt upon Himself, and therefore as soon as we take Him as our sin-bearer, we have again perfect access to God and to His strengthening, delivering, and transforming grace. We read in Galatians 3:13: *Christ redeemed us from the curse of the law, having become a curse for us: for it is written, Cursed is every one that hangeth on a tree.* And we read in 2 Corinthians 5:21: *Him who knew no sin [God] made to be sin on our behalf; that we might become the righteousness of God in him.*

One day, some years ago, I heard a man who was raised from childhood as a thief; he had spent years in prison in various states in the Union and in other lands, but he had come to see that God loved him, vile as he was. He learned that Jesus had died for him and he told the story of how faith in this Christ, Christ Jesus, had opened the way to God and salvation for him. Thousands upon thousands could tell essentially similar stories. Christ Jesus is beyond question, on the testimony of countless competent witnesses, a cure for the guilt of sin.

This last week I stood on the street waiting for a car, and a man stepped up to me to talk to me. I thought at first he was going to talk about the common subjects of the day, as so many do. But instead of that he at once asked, "Do you think a man can sin away the day of grace?"

I looked into his face and into the depths of his eyes, yes, into the depths of his soul. I saw the anxiety and sorrow that were in his heart, so I asked him, "Why do you ask?"

Then he opened his breaking heart to me right there on the street, and I was able to speak to him of our glorious gospel, and how according to it, all our sins have been laid on Jesus Christ and settled. I told him how Jesus had said, *Him that cometh to me I will in no wise cast out* (John 6:37). A new light and a new hope came into the man's eyes, and when I left him to take the car, there was a smile of peace upon his face. No other gospel than the gospel of the Christ who was crucified for our sins will bring a profound sense of sins forgiven to a man. No other gospel will assure him that no matter how many or how great his sins may have been, there is pardon for him on the ground of the atoning death of Jesus Christ. With that single but all-sufficient ground, he has access to God.

But the Lord Jesus Christ saves not only from the guilt of sin, He also saves from the power of sin. This man of whom I spoke a few moments ago as having been brought up in childhood as a thief, who had spent years in prison in this country and other lands, told of the desperate struggles he had made to break away from the power of sin and be a man. But failure followed failure, and despair stared the man in the face. Then he took Jesus Christ as his personal Savior, and the fetters of sin, the fetters of the appetite for drink, the fetters of impurity and profanity, and a host of evil habits were snapped away in a moment.

> The Lord Jesus Christ saves not only from the guilt of sin, He also saves from the power of sin.

This is only one case in thousands. Christ is a sure cure for sin, a sure deliverer from the power of sin, no matter how deep-seated and desperate the case may be. We read in 1 Timothy 1:15: *This is a faithful saying, and worthy of all acceptation, that Christ Jesus came into the world to save sinners;* then Paul added his own experience: *of whom I am chief.* This statement of Paul's was true, of course. Every statement in the Bible is true, but this particular statement that Jesus Christ came to save the chief of sinners, if he will only put his trust in Him, I have seen verified in countless instances.

One morning at the close of the morning service in the People's Church in Minneapolis, of which I was then pastor, one of my deacons stepped up to a gentleman and said, "Are you a Christian?"

"No sir," he replied.

"Why not?" the deacon asked.

"I am too great a sinner to be saved," was the reply.

To his amazement, the deacon exclaimed, "Thank God!" Then the deacon turned to me on the platform and called, "Brother Torrey, here is a man who says he is too great a sinner to be saved. Thank God!"

The gentleman looked more bewildered than ever. I stepped down to him and asked, "Is what the deacon says true?"

"Yes," he said, "I am too great a sinner to be saved."

Though he had the appearance of a gentleman, he was a great sinner. He had run away and left his wife in Toronto, Canada, and was squandering his manhood and his money in gambling in Minneapolis. He had lost thirty-five thousand dollars at the gaming table just the week before.

When he said he was too great a sinner to be saved, I said, "Let me show you something," and opening my Bible to 1 Timothy 1:15, I asked him to read.

And he read, "*This is a faithful saying, and worthy of all acceptation, that Christ Jesus came into the world to save sinners; of whom I am chief.*" Then he said, "Well, I am chief."

"Well," I said, "then it means you."

"It is a precious promise," he said.

"Will you accept it now?" I asked.

He said, "I will."

I said, "Let us kneel down and tell God so." We knelt side by side and prayed, and when he rose, he knew that God had forgiven all his sins. He left the following week for the Northwest, and I lost track of him for nearly a year, for he never wrote to me. Then I learned that he had returned to St. Paul and was working every night for the salvation of others. He had brought his wife from Toronto, and they were reunited and so happy in their new life that they had adopted a little girl from an orphanage to make their home complete.

No man need continue in sin. God has provided a cure. The Lord Jesus Himself tells us what that cure is: *If the Son* [the Son of God, Jesus Himself] *therefore shall make you free, ye shall be free indeed* (John 8:36).

Jesus Christ Is the Cure for Sin in Society

Jesus Christ is not only the cure for sin in the individual, He is also the cure for sin in society as a whole. Men propose various remedies for the cure of sin and crime in the world. The best of those remedies will prove only partially effective. Whatever prohibition laws may accomplish, they will never banish sin or crime. I believe in prohibition. I believe it was a good thing; it is a great thing in many ways, as many of us know from personal observation and experience, when the prohibition enactment went into effect in this land. But prohibition does not banish sin, and it never will. There has been more sin and crime in our country since the adoption of prohibition than before. Prohibition is not to blame for that.

There are numerous causes, prominent among which is the fact that we are reaping the aftermath of the war (World War I). Oh, war is a hellish thing, a most damnable thing. Crime would have been even worse, far worse than it is, if it had not been for prohibition. But while prohibition is not to blame for the increase of sin and crime, the increase of sin and crime after the adoption of prohibition does show that prohibition will not cure sin. Neither will any other kind of external law cure sin, no matter how wise and beneficent the law may be. Jesus Christ alone, the personal Jesus Christ, is the cure for sin in the individual and also the cure for sin and crime in the state, in the home, and in society in general. His coming again will utterly banish sin and crime from the earth, so that righteousness and the knowledge of the Lord shall cover the earth *as the waters cover the sea* (Isaiah 11:9).

Jesus, then, is the cure for all sin in every aspect of its working.

Jesus Christ Is the Cure for Unbelief

The next greatest evil to sin is unbelief. Indeed, the two go hand in hand; where sin reigns unbelief reigns, where unbelief reigns sin reigns. Unbelief begets sin, and sin fosters further unbelief. Undermine the faith of men in the Bible, the God of the Bible, and the Christ of the Bible, and a carnival of lust, greed, passion, hate, dishonesty, murder, and war with all its accompanying horrors is the result. Increasing unbelief is one of the chief causes, the one fundamental cause, of lust, crime, immorality, immodesty, indecency, lawlessness, robbery, and murder that is sweeping over our land today. Our schools, colleges, and universities have been undermining faith in the Bible, the God of the Bible, and the Christ of the Bible, and we are reaping the harvest, and an awful harvest it is.

> Unbelief begets sin, and sin fosters further unbelief.

The things I read in the newspapers about men and women being held up and robbed every night, and sometimes murdered, are depressing. But to a man who looks ahead with a clear eye, they are not as depressing as what one sees everywhere of the immodest, bold, shameless conduct of the rising generation, the conduct of our high school boys and girls and, yes, with our elementary school boys and girls. Unbelief has come into our schools and homes like a flood; many of our boys and girls are not in Sunday school, studying the one Book of all other books that makes for noble character and good citizenship. Instead, they are off spending the weekend in the mountains, boys and girls together, and down at the seashore, watching and joining in immodest parades and various other things. They are also at the movies by the thousands, movies whose chief attraction is often indecency.

Take any daily paper, and you will find that it advertises indecent movies with grossly suggestive pictures to allure the young, advertisements of such a character that not many years ago, a paper would have been prosecuted if it had dared to publish them. Even the YWCA, that is supposed to be a Christian institution and "an arm of the church," takes hiking parties of young girls on the Lord's Day; it takes them away from home and Sunday school and church to spend the weekend in a canyon. A further spread of infidelity in our city would bring more profit to the bootleggers, gambling houses, and brothels than a governmental subsidy.

But men say, "That may be so, but I cannot help my unbelief. If I cannot believe, I cannot, and that is all there is to it."

No, that is not all there is to it. There is a cure, a sure cure for unbelief; the cure is Jesus Christ. Go to Jesus Christ. Tell Him your unbelief. Make a clean breast of it. Tell Him you cannot believe in the Bible; you cannot believe in God; you cannot believe in Him the way Christians claim to believe in Him. But, tell Him also that if the Bible is true, you want to know it; if there is a God, you want to know it and want to know Him. Tell Him that if He is the Son of God, you want to know that too. And tell Him that if He will show you, then you will accept Him as your Savior and surrender to Him as your Lord;

you will confess Him as such before the world. Then take the words of Jesus as they have been recorded in the four Gospels, and take in particular the Gospel of John and read it honestly, looking for light and obeying the light as fast as you get it. Your skepticism and your unbelief will soon vanish. My friend, you may not be to blame for your unbelief, but you will be to blame if you continue in it, for I have pointed out a cure. Thousands have tried this cure. It has never failed in one single instance.

For years, I stood in the pulpit of the Moody Church in Chicago and challenged unbelievers to come to me, and I would show them a rational cure for their unbelief, and if it did not succeed in any case, I would let the unbeliever speak from that platform. Many came, but there was never a case of failure, not a single one where men really took the remedy suggested.

One night a man was brought to me. He had boasted very loudly that he wanted to ask me a few questions. Well, I asked *him* a few. I asked him if he thought there was an absolute difference between right and wrong.

He said, "Yes."

"Well," I said, "then you ought to take your stand and follow the right wherever it carries you. Will you do it?"

He tried to hedge, but I held him to it, and finally he said, "Yes."

Then I asked him if he knew that there was no God, or if he knew that God did not answer prayer. He replied, "No, I do not know it. In fact, I think there is a Supreme Being." But he added that he did not believe that this Supreme Being answered prayer.

"Well, do you know He does not answer prayer?" I asked.

"No," he replied, "I do not know that He does not."

"Well," I said, "I know that He does, but I do not ask you to take my word for it; try it for yourself. Here is a possible clue – it may be that God answers prayer. If you are as honest as you say you are in your search for truth, you will try this clue and discover what may be in it. Will you pray this prayer? 'O God, if there be any God, show me if Jesus Christ is Your Son or not; if You will show me that He is, I promise to accept Him as my Savior and confess Him as such before the world.'"

He tried now to hedge and crawl more than ever. He wanted to ask me what life was and many other irrelevant questions. But I held him to the point. I showed him that what was wrong was that he did not care to pray. But at last, in desperation he got down on his knees and in his excitement kicked over a chair and blurted out the words of a prayer.

"Now," I said, "will you just take the Gospel of John and read it, honestly looking for light, and come back in two weeks and tell me the result?"

"Yes, I will," he said. But he never came back. Why not? You know. He did not want to be cured of his unbelief. He wanted unbelief because he wanted sin.

But many did come back, and they all came back cured. I have been making this same offer for many years now in many cities, many states, and many lands, and there has never been a single case of failure yet. No man has yet come back who has been able to tell me that he had taken the remedy and remained a skeptic. Now, if you doubt that cure, try it yourself.

Jesus Christ Is the Cure for Poverty

The third evil I desire to refer to is poverty. Jesus Christ is the cure for poverty. I stand with Henry George when he says poverty is an evil.[7] Men may get good out of poverty; many men have gotten good out of poverty, but poverty is an evil. It is all

---

7   Henry George was an American political economist and journalist in nineteenth-century America.

very well for philosophers like Seneca,[8] whom Ingersoll[9] lauded and exalted above Paul and Jesus Christ, to write about the excellencies of poverty when they themselves are squandering, as Seneca himself did, vast fortunes in the most extravagant luxury. Such philosophy may suit a reckless discharger of verbal pyrotechnics such as Colonel Ingersoll, but it will not suit honest, thinking people who love their kind and keep their eyes open. Poverty is an evil.

When I walk through the homes of the poor in various cities of this and other countries, I see the crowding, breathe the poisonous air, and hear the curses, oaths, and obscenities that greet the ears of the innocent children from the day they open their eyes to the day they are carried out to the potter's field. When I hear and see these things, I feel like saying, "Cursed be poverty." Poverty is an evil and I hate it. I hate it not only for myself but I also hate it for the sake of those who suffer from it. I cannot walk among the homes of the poor without heartache, and I do not wish to. Poverty is an evil; Jesus Christ is the cure.

Jesus Christ Is the Cure for Poverty with the Individual
First of all, Jesus Christ is the cure for poverty in this life. There is no guarantee that if a man comes to Christ he will become a man of wealth in this present life. That is not desirable for most men. Indeed, very few men have great wealth in this life who are not spoiled by it. But there is a guarantee that if one comes to Christ, really believing in Him as Savior, and surrendering absolutely to Him as Lord and Master, their every real need will be supplied.

---

8 Seneca was a Roman philosopher and statesman whose lasting contribution has been to the school of stoicism, which taught that virtue is the only good for human beings.

9 Robert Green Ingersoll was an American lawyer, writer, and orator during the Golden Age of Freethought who campaigned in defense of agnosticism.

Jesus Christ Himself says in Matthew 6:33, *But seek ye first the kingdom of God, and his righteousness; and all these things shall be added unto you.* And the *all these things* are the things spoken of in the verses immediately preceding: food, drink, clothing, and the necessities of daily life. This statement of Jesus Christ's is true. I have watched the testing of it under abnormally trying circumstances for forty years, and I have never known a case of failure. I have known cases of seeming failure, but when examined closely, I have found that the failure was not in the promise of God but because people did not meet the conditions of the promise.

Paul says in Philippians 4:19, *My God shall supply all your need according to his riches in glory by Christ Jesus.* That great promise is also true when you meet the conditions stated in the context. I have seen these promises tested again and again in the most unpromising circumstances, and neither of them has ever failed. It has often seemed as if they were going to fail, but they never have.

I have known many people who were in the most abject poverty who have attained to positions of comfort and plenty through accepting Jesus Christ. Many of them go trooping by in my memory as I speak. All over the city of Chicago and all over the country, there are people who have been lifted from poverty to plenty and affluence by the influence of one church, the Moody Church in Chicago. Not that this church has given them money, but the church has brought them to Christ, and Christ has brought them to plenty. The same is true of many churches throughout the land. As a matter of demonstrated fact, Jesus Christ is the cure for poverty with the individual.

Jesus Christ Is the Cure for Poverty in the Life to Come
The man or woman who accepts Jesus Christ becomes a child of God, and if a child, then an heir, an heir of God and a joint

heir with Christ (John 1:12; Romans 8:17). If the poorest beggar in the land were to accept Jesus Christ, that beggar would become at once an heir to estates whose magnificence far surpasses those of all the multimillionaires in the land. I pass by and behold the mansions of the rich in many cities; I enter and go through the magnificent palaces of kings and emperors, as I have done in many lands, and I say all this is nothing, nothing compared to what I am soon to have.

Oh, I invite all to untold riches. For the child of God there is just a little time before he receives *an inheritance incorruptible, and undefiled, and that fadeth not away.*

Jesus Christ Is the Cure for Poverty in Society at Large
How earnestly and fruitlessly social philosophers have sought for a cure for poverty. I think Henry George has come the nearest of anyone to hitting upon a cure that would be effective and practicable. But I confess I do not expect to ever see it put into operation in the large way it would be necessary to have it accomplish any real and permanent good. And even if it were put into operation, I would not expect to see all the results that its more sanguine supporters imagine would follow. There would still be poverty, because there would still be cunning greed on the one side and improvidence, laziness, and waste on the other side.

But when Jesus comes again to reign, He will banish poverty. Love will reign. The lion and the lamb will lie down together, and the lamb will not be inside the lion, as is now so often the case (Isaiah 11:6). No more poverty, no more oppression, no more commercial warfare, no more ravaging of the strong robbing the weak when Jesus Christ comes. Equality, fraternity, and plenty will reign everywhere.

People ask me why I'm looking forward to the second coming of the Lord Jesus Christ. I long for the speedy coming of

Jesus Christ for many reasons. But one reason is that I go out and see the poor thousands and tens of thousands in the great cities of our land. I see the human hogs that dominate the business, politics, and society of our day who trample the weak under their feet and into the mud in their gluttonous desire to get at their garbage. I feel like crying, "How long, O Lord, how long? Come, Lord Jesus. Come quickly." This is my only hope for those who are deprived in the present, mad scramble that we call business. But that is an all-sufficient hope. He is coming! And when He comes, society will be reconstructed from the bottom up. The principle that governs human life will no longer be competition – that is, "every man for himself and the devil take the hindmost." But when He comes, the governing principle of all society will be *love your neighbor as yourself,* and poverty, lack, and oppression will then be no more forever.

Jesus Christ is the cure for poverty. If you wish to see poverty done away with, enlist in the army of Jesus Christ.

Jesus Christ Is the Cure for Sickness

The next evil is sickness. Some people consider sickness a blessing, and God undoubtedly does make a blessing out of sickness for some of us. I have had sicknesses and pains for which I have thanked God. But if I read my Bible correctly, sickness was a curse, and it belongs properly to the devil's kingdom and not God's. And I notice that most of the people who consider sickness a blessing are perfectly willing that the other fellow should enjoy all the blessings of this kind. If the blessing happens to come their way, they are willing to take all kinds of bitter pills and nauseating potions to rid themselves of this highly esteemed blessing. In plain, unvarnished English, sickness is a great evil. Jesus Christ is the cure for sickness.

A PERFECT CURE FOR POVERTY AND ALL OTHER EVILS OF THE DAY

Jesus Christ Is the Cure for Sickness in This Present Life

The general rule of God regarding His children is that God wishes them to be well, and Jesus Christ makes them well when they trust Him to do it. I am not going into the fine and disputed points about divine healing and the faith cure, but I know from personal experience and careful observation for many years that the Lord Jesus Christ, who was raised from the dead and ascended to the right hand of the Father, has all power in heaven and on earth and does cure sickness today. Jesus Christ, the risen Son of God, has cured many a man and woman who has been hopelessly sick for years and whom all physicians failed to heal.

Jesus Christ's Healing Power Will Be Manifested in the Life to Come

God's dearest and purest and noblest children do get sick and die in this life; but in the life that lies ahead, there will be no death, no sickness, and no pain. There will be, however, in that other world for those who reject Christ in this world plenty of sickness, pain, and eternal death – endless dying. Oh, sick one, come to Jesus. He is the cure for sickness.

Time fails me to mention other evils such as bereavement, disappointment, bitterness of heart, despair, and death for which Jesus and only Jesus is the cure. Jesus Christ is the cure for every evil known to man. He stands now with outstretched hands as He did that day in Capernaum when He uttered the words of our text. And He calls to us as He did to them: *Come unto me, all ye that labour and are heavy laden, and I will give you rest. Take my yoke upon you, and learn of me; for I am meek and lowly in heart: and ye shall find rest unto your souls. For my yoke is easy and my burden is light* (Matthew 11:28-30).

Chapter 12

Jesus Is the Christ, the Son of God

These are written, that ye may believe that Jesus is the Christ, the Son of God; and that believing ye may have life in his name. (John 20:31)

My subject here is "Jesus is the Christ, the Son of God." The text is in John 20:31: *These are written, that ye may believe that Jesus is the Christ, the Son of God; and that believing ye may have life in his name.*

This text declares that Jesus is the Christ, the Son of God, and that everyone who really believes that fact obtains eternal life by so believing. Read it again: *These are written, that ye may believe that Jesus is the Christ, the Son of God; and that believing ye may have life in his name.*

Jesus Is the Christ, the Son of God

How do we know that Jesus is the Christ, the Son of God?

First of all, we know that Jesus is the Christ, the Son of God, by a careful and candid study of the Gospel of John. John says,

These are written, that ye may believe that Jesus is the Christ, the Son of God; and that believing ye may have life in his name. In other words, in his Gospel, John presents the evidence that Jesus is the Christ, the Son of God. We cannot take up that evidence here, nor do we need to. Any of you may examine it for yourself; if you will candidly read the evidence as John presents it, with a sincere desire to know the truth and with an earnest determination to obey the truth when discovered, you will know with certainty that Jesus is the Christ, the Son of God, even before you finish John's Gospel.

I challenge any man to study the Gospel of John with a candid mind, with a sincere desire to know the truth and a willingness to obey it when it is found, and to come to any other conclusion than without doubt that Jesus is the very Christ of God, and the very Son of God. I have seen men try again and again; many were skeptics or even thoroughgoing agnostics when they began, and in every case where any man has pursued the truth with a willingness to obey it at any cost, he has become a believer that Jesus is the Christ, the Son of God, by the time he completed the Gospel. The result has been the same in every instance. Every one of them has come to see that Jesus is the Christ, the Son of God, and by believing in Him as such, has obtained eternal life. I suppose I could stand here by the hour and tell you of specific instances that have come under my own personal observation. Let me give you only one.

When I was holding meetings in Wellington, New Zealand, I spoke to business and professional men during the noon hour in one of the theaters. At the close of one of these meetings, a prominent traveling man came to me; he was said to be the most prominent traveling man in New Zealand. He said, "Charlie George (he was one of the proprietors of the leading department store in the city) thinks I ought to have a talk with you, but you can't help me."

I said, "What is the trouble?"

He replied, "I am an agnostic, and you can't help me."

"Well," I said, "I have helped a good many agnostics, and perhaps I can help you." Then I continued. "What do you believe anyhow?"

He said, "I don't believe anything."

I said, "Do you not believe that there is an absolute difference between right and wrong?"

"Oh yes," he said, "I do believe that."

"Well," I said, "you do believe something after all. That is all that I believed to begin with, and that is enough for anyone to believe to begin with." Then I said, "If you have some of anything and want more, what do you do?"

"Why," he said, "I use what I have."

I said, "That is right. If you have some muscle and want more muscle, what do you do?"

He said, "I use the muscle I have."

"If you have some memory and want a better memory, what do you do?"

"I use the memory I have."

"If you have some money and want more money, what do you do?"

"I use the money I have."

"All right," I said, "you have some faith. You believe there is an absolute difference between right and wrong. You want more. Will you use what you have? You say you believe that there is an absolute difference between right and wrong. Will you use that faith? Will you take your stand upon the right to follow it wherever it carries you, at any cost?"

With a little hesitation, he said, "Yes, I will do that, but you can't help me, you are just wasting your time."

"Now," I said, "do you know that there is no God?"

"No," he said, "I don't know there is no God. I don't know anything about it."

"Well," I said, "I know that there is a God, but that won't do you any good. Do you know that God does not answer prayer?"

"No," he said, "I don't know that God doesn't answer prayer. I don't believe that He does, but I don't know that He doesn't."

"Well," I said, "I know that He does, but that won't do you any good. But you know the method of modern science. The method of modern science is this: that whenever you find a possible clue to knowledge, you follow that clue to discover what there may be in it. You don't have to know that there is anything in it. You simply follow it to find out what there may be in it."

"Yes," he said, "that is right."

"Well now," I said, "are you willing to apply this method of modern science to religious investigation? You admit that there may be a God, and He might answer prayer. Here then is a possible clue to knowledge. Will you follow it to find out what there may be in it? Will you pray this prayer? 'Oh, God, if there be any God, show me if Jesus Christ is Your Son or not, and if You show me that He is, I promise to accept Him as my Savior and confess Him as such before the world.'"

"Yes," he said in a half-laughing way, "I'll do that too, but it won't do any good; you can't help me, you are just wasting your time."

"Well," I replied, "I have helped a good many, and perhaps I can help you. Now, just one thing more. John says in John 20:31, *These are written, that ye may believe that Jesus is the Christ, the Son of God; and that believing ye may have life in his name.* John presents to you in his Gospel the evidence that Jesus is the Christ, the Son of God. Will you take the evidence and read it? I don't ask you to believe it; I don't want you to even try to believe it; I simply want you to be willing to be convinced. Will you take the Gospel and read it with an open mind?"

"Oh," he said, "I have read it."

"Yes," I said, "but I want you to read it in a new way. Begin at the first chapter and the first verse and read on verse after verse until you finish the Gospel. Don't read too many verses at any one time. Pay careful attention to what you read, and each time before you read, offer this prayer: 'Oh God, if there be any God, show me what of truth there is in these verses I am about to read, and what you show me to be true, I promise to take my stand upon.'"

Rather languidly and wearily he said, "Yes, I will do that too, but it won't do any good."

Then I went over what he had agreed to do and got him to promise me he would write to me the result.

Several weeks passed. I left Wellington and went to Christ Church and from Christ Church to Dunedin. After I had been a few days in Dunedin, a lady called at the house where I was stopping and asked to see me. When I entered the reception room, she rose and walked toward me with a letter in her hand, which she held out to me. She said, "I have a letter from my husband, and it is the queerest letter I ever received. I don't understand it, but he said I could show it to you." She handed me the letter, and I took it and read it. It was from this man. It began: "My dear wife: I think I have been converted. I am not sure yet, and I don't wish you to tell anyone until I am sure, but you can show this letter to your pastor and to Dr. Torrey, for it was he who spoke to me in Wellington."

That man emerged as a Christian, as a believer in Jesus as the Christ, the Son of God, and in the Bible as the Word of God. When we arrived in England, his mother, who was a very prominent woman in public life there, wrote to Mr. Alexander to thank us for what we had done for her son in New Zealand. Any one of you can try it for yourself. The result always has been the same and always will be the same. There has never been an exception.

In the second place, we know that Jesus is the Christ, the Son of God, because that is what Jesus Himself claimed to be, and God set the stamp of His endorsement on His claim by raising Him from the dead. That Jesus claimed to be the Christ, the Son of God, the Son of God in a unique sense, in a sense that no other man who ever walked this earth was the Son of God, is unquestionable.

In Mark 12:6 our Lord Jesus draws a contrast between Himself and all the prophets of the old dispensation, even the greatest of those. He says that while they were merely servants, He is the Son, the one and only Son of God. In John 10:30 Jesus went so far as to say, *I and the Father are one.* In John 14:9 He even dared to say, *He that hath seen me hath seen the Father.* In John 5:23 He goes so far as to say, *All men should honour the Son, even as they honour the Father.* Such was Jesus' often-repeated claim.

This was an astounding claim to make. If the claim was not true, it was an utterly and shamefully blasphemous claim. The Jews put Jesus Christ to death on a charge of blasphemy for making this claim. And if this claim of Jesus was not true and Jesus was not the Christ, the Son of God, the Son of God in a sense that no other is the Son of God, then the Jews did the right thing according to their own God-given law in putting Him to death on the charge of blasphemy, except they should have put Him to death by stoning and not by crucifixion.

You cannot deny the deity of Jesus without also justifying the Jews in putting Him to death. If you are a Unitarian and are also logical, you must justify the putting to death of Jesus

Christ. But before the Jewish authorities put Him to death, Jesus said to them that God would set the stamp of His endorsement upon His claim for which they were putting Him to death by raising Him from the dead. Put Him to death – they did; lay Him in Joseph's sepulcher – they did; roll the stone to the door of the sepulcher – they did; seal the stone with the Roman seal (which to break was death) – they did.

But when the appointed hour came, just as Jesus had foretold, the quickening breath of God swept through that sleeping clay, and God raised Him triumphant over death and grave. In so doing, He proclaimed to all future generations, and to us, more clearly than if He proclaimed it from the open heavens above Los Angeles today: "This man is what He claimed to be; He is the Christ; He is the Son of God. All men should honor Him even as they honor Me, the Father."

I have proved time and again from this platform that the resurrection of Jesus from the dead is the best proven fact of history, and the absolutely certain resurrection of the Lord Jesus Christ demonstrates that He is the Christ, the Son of God.

In the third place, we know that Jesus is the Christ, the Son of God, by His influence upon all subsequent history. That Jesus Christ claimed to be the Christ, the Son of God, in an entirely unique sense, as we have already seen, is not even an honest question. But that Jesus claimed to be the Christ, the Son of God, a divine person to be honored and worshipped, even as God the Father is honored and worshipped, does not prove that He really was so. But it does prove that He either was the Son of God in a unique sense, as He claimed to be, or that He was the most daring, blasphemous, and outrageous impostor that ever walked this earth, or that He was one of the most hopeless lunatics that ever disgraced humanity by his mental imbecility.

The modern Unitarian position, the position also of some preachers who do not call themselves Unitarians but orthodox and evangelical, is that Jesus was not a divine person. They believe that He was the Son of God only in the sense that we are all sons of God; they believe He was a good man, perhaps the best man who ever lived on this earth, but this is the very culmination of irrationality and intellectual absurdity. Whatever Jesus was, He was not a good man; that is to say, if He were not God as He claimed to be, He was not good but was one of the most outrageous impostors or one of the most hopeless lunatics that ever walked this earth.

Now let me ask each one of you a question. Was the influence of Jesus of Nazareth upon subsequent history the influence of an impostor? Only one whose own heart is corrupted by imposture and fraud would think for one moment of asserting that. Let me ask you a second question. Was the influence of Jesus of Nazareth upon subsequent history the influence of a lunatic? Only a lunatic would venture to assert that. Here then we are – He's not a lunatic, not an impostor, then beyond question He is the Christ, the Son of God, God manifest in the flesh.

In the fourth place, we know that Jesus is the Christ, the Son of God, by the divine power that He displays today. Jesus displayed divine power when He was here on earth. He displayed divine power when He stilled the tempest and calmed the waves by His word, saying, *Peace, be still,* and there was a great calm. He displayed divine power when He called Lazarus, who had been dead four days, from the grave, and Lazarus came forth. He displayed divine power when He turned water into wine. He displayed divine power when He fed five thousand men, besides women and children, with five small loaves and two small fish and had more left over when He was through than when He began, which was a creative act.

Over and over again He displayed divine power when He was here on earth. But we do not need to go that far back into the history of His life upon earth, nearly nineteen hundred years ago, to find Him displaying divine power. He displays divine power today. He raises the dead today. He raises men and women who are dead in trespasses and sins into spiritual life and power and victory. He does something far more wonderful than turning water into wine. He turns outrageous sinners into glorious saints.

He turned a Jerry McAuley, a miserable, contemptible, low-down river thief, an inmate of Sing Sing Prison, into Jerry McAuley, the apostle of life to the outcasts of New York. He was so honored when he came to die in the very city where he had been a water thief, that the best people of New York gathered by the thousands at his funeral to do honor to his blessed memory.

Jesus Christ turned Sam Hadley, a fugitive from justice with 138 counts of forgery against him, and a hopeless barrelhouse bum, into Sam Hadley, one of the most lovable men and self-sacrificing lovers of his fellow men I ever knew. I once met him in Washington as the honored guest in the home of the postmaster general of the United States of America.

Jesus Christ also changed William S. Jacoby, a drunkard at nine, an antagonizer at fifteen, a criminal at nineteen, and a companion of thugs, a desperado in Omaha, twice dishonorably discharged from the regular army. He was invited to join the Jesse James Gang, unanimously chosen chief of a gang of desperados in the Leavenworth Federal Prison, riding through the streets of Omaha and firing his revolver out of the window of a cab at everything he passed. Jesus turned that man into the Reverend William S. Jacoby, the most loved man in Chicago, the dearest and truest friend I ever had. He was the most truly Christlike man I ever knew.

Yes, and He changed me. I will not tell you from what, but at least from hopeless bondage to glorious liberty, and from awful death to exultant life. Yes, Jesus is surely the Christ, the

Son of God. There is no possibility of honest and intelligent doubt of that.

The Result of Believing Jesus Is the Christ

Now let us look at the result of believing that Jesus is the Christ, the Son of God. What will be the result? Read the text again – *These are written, that ye may believe that Jesus is the Christ, the Son of God; and that believing ye may have life in his name.*

First, the result will be that the one who believes that Jesus is the Christ, the Son of God, will obtain eternal life. This is all that anyone needs to do to obtain eternal life, that greatest of all gifts; all the wealth, splendor, honor, glory, and pleasures of this world are as nothing in comparison. All that anyone has to do to obtain this wondrous gift is to believe that Jesus is the Christ, the Son of God.

> Anyone may have eternal life in the twinkling of an eye by just believing that Jesus is the Christ, the Son of God.

Anyone may have eternal life in the twinkling of an eye by just believing that Jesus is the Christ, the Son of God.

Read the text again – *These are written, that ye may believe that Jesus is the Christ, the Son of God; and that believing ye may have life in his name.* Then note another verse – *For God so loved the world, that he gave his only begotten Son, that whosoever believeth in him should not perish, but have everlasting life* (John 3:16). You may be a drunkard, a thief, an embezzler, or a forger. You may be a man or woman who is disgraced by divorce; you may be the guilty party, or you may be an outrageous blasphemer. You may have a polluted imagination and a rotten heart; you may be the victim of the lowest and vilest passions that ever cursed a man or woman; you may be anybody or anything. But, believe that Jesus is the Christ, the Son of God, and eternal life is instantly yours. Oh, how often I have seen men and women of all kinds and conditions and nationalities receive eternal life in an instant by simply believing that Jesus is the Christ, the Son of God.

Of course, your belief must be real faith. The faith that John speaks of here is not a mere intellectual opinion. John never uses the word *faith* in that sense. No man ever obtained eternal life by merely having an orthodox opinion of Jesus.

When Jesus was here on earth, the demons held a perfectly orthodox opinion of Him. They cried out (even before men saw it and confessed it), *I know thee who thou art, the Holy One of God.* The devil holds a perfectly orthodox opinion of Christ. He knows, and only too well for his own comfort, that Jesus is the Christ, the Son of God. He does not teach it, but he knows it. He gets men to teach that Jesus is not the Christ, the Son of God, very God of very God, because *he is a liar, and the father of it* (John 8:44). He gets men to teach that Jesus is a good man, a great example, but not divine, and that He does not save by the shedding of His blood but by His example and His teaching, for the devil *is a liar, and the father of it.*

But all the time the devil knows that Jesus is the Christ, the Son of God. He knows that someday he will be forced to bow his knee to Jesus and *confess that Jesus Christ is Lord, to the glory of God the Father* (Philippians 2:11). Yes, the devil believes in that sense that Jesus is the Christ, the Son of God, but that belief does not save him from going to the everlasting fire prepared for him and his angels. No, the faith that saves is real faith, a faith with the heart. As Paul puts it in Romans 10:9-10: *If thou shalt confess with thy mouth Jesus as Lord, and shalt believe in thy heart that God raised him from the dead, thou shalt be saved: for with the heart man believeth unto righteousness; and with the mouth confession is made unto salvation.*

What is heart faith, real faith, saving faith, eternal-life-giving faith? Heart faith, real faith, saving faith, eternal-life-giving faith is the faith that not only enlightens the mind but also governs the will and the feelings and the conduct. It is the faith that leads to action in accordance with the truth believed. To believe with the heart that Jesus is the Christ, the Son of God, will lead you to act in accordance with the fact that Jesus is the Christ, the Son of God.

The word *Christ* is really a Greek word and means "Anointed One." It means just the same as the Hebrew word *Messiah*, which means "Anointed King." To believe with the heart that Jesus is the Christ will lead you to enthrone Jesus as King in your heart and to surrender the whole control and conduct of your life to Him. To believe with the heart that Jesus is the Son of God will lead you to surrender every thought to His control, so that if the whole world of German scholarship and English scholarship and Scottish scholarship and American scholarship should say one thing and the Lord Jesus should say another, you would believe Jesus against the whole crowd.

If the great and widely respected Dean Shailer Mathews and the scholarly Professor Case and a whole bevy of self-styled scholars, some with more degrees after their names than they have real sound sense in their heads and humility in their hearts, should say one thing and Jesus Christ should say another thing, I would believe the glorious Son of God against the whole pretentious but pitiful pack. And if you believe with your heart that Jesus is the Christ, the Son of God, you will accept Him as your divine Savior. He purchased forgiveness for you by dying in your place on the cross, for that is what He said He did (Matthew 20:28), and by His resurrection power, He can set you free from the power of sin today, for that is what He offers to do (John 8:34-36).

Once more, if you believe that Jesus is the Christ, the Son of God, you will bow down before Him and honor Him, even as you honor God the Father. You will worship Him as the divine person He claims to be and that you know Him to be. You will do what Thomas did when at last after many doubts, he was brought to faith to believe that Jesus was the Christ, the Son of God, by seeing the risen Christ. You too will fall down upon your knees and look up into His blessed, glorious, divine face and cry to Him, "My Lord and my God," and you will obtain eternal life the moment you do. Will you do it now?

Chapter 13

Which Shall We Believe: God or Man?

For what if some did not believe? shall their unbelief make the faith of God without effect? God forbid: yea, let God be true, but every man a liar.
(Romans 3:3-4)

What I say now will save some of you, eternally and gloriously save you. But alas, it will also lead to the eternal doom and destruction of some of you. It will save some of you because you will listen to the truth, and as a result of your listening attentively and honestly, you will take the steps today that will lead to your salvation right here and now. But what I say will also lead to the eternal doom and destruction of some of you because you will not listen to the truth but will harden your hearts against it and reject it. Thus, this very sermon that might have saved you, if you had taken it to heart, will imperil you in the day of judgment. Truth observed saves, truth rejected damns. Our Lord Jesus says in John 12:48, *He that rejecteth me, and receiveth not my words, hath one that judgeth him: the word that I have spoken, the same shall judge him in the last day.*

And the truth I bring has in it a peculiar saving power if you will only take it to heart and believe it and obey it. It also has in it peculiar power to bring condemnation and doom and destruction to those who refuse to listen and thereby reject it.

My subject is "Which Shall We Believe, God or Man?" You will find my text in Romans 3:3-4: *For what if some did not believe? shall their unbelief make the faith of God without effect? God forbid: yea, let God be true, but every man a liar.*

God's Word Better Than Man's

We live in a day when men are disposed to put great faith in what men say, especially what learned men say, but very little faith or no faith at all in what God says. Let some great man of science announce a discovery, and no matter how astonishing or even incredible that discovery may seem to be, no matter how much there is about it that we cannot understand, we believe it at once. But let a man find something in the Word of God that is contrary to his preconceived notions, outside his own experience, that he cannot understand, or something that for one reason or another appears incredible at first glance, he discards it at once. Tell men what great men say, and they accept it at once. Tell men what the Bible says, and they look wise and shrug their shoulders and say, "Yes, but I don't think so. This is what I think." And yet, tell them what some great scientist or some leading literary critic or some brilliant but erratic preacher says, and they think that settles it, and it must be so. What utter foolishness!

The opinion of the greatest scientist that ever lived, the greatest philosopher, the most learned Hebrew or Greek scholar, or the most brilliant pulpit orator is of no value whatever against the Word of the infinitely wise and eternally truthful God, and against the Word of the God *that cannot lie* and is never mistaken. The opinion of all the wise men on earth is of no weight whatever against the Word of God. One short sentence from God's sure Word is worth whole volumes of man's vain speculations: *Let God be found true, but every man a liar.* The man who believes any man before he believes God is a fool. The man who believes any company of men before he believes God is a fool. The man who believes God before he believes the whole world is a truly wise man.

The Bible is the Word of God. That can be proven by many unanswerable proofs. I have proven it time and again from this platform. For eighteen centuries and more, the opinions of scientists and philosophers have come and gone – regarded as the final and absolute wisdom today, but as sheerest folly tomorrow. But the teachings of this Book have stood fast amid the wreckage of centuries of man's thinking. The experience of eighteen centuries proves that the man who relies on the Bible is wise. The man who throws the Bible overboard at any point and turns to any other source of "light and leading" always misses it. He always has missed it for eighteen centuries; he always will miss it for all the centuries to come. The truly wise man is the man who always believes this Book before any man, scientist, philosopher, literary scholar, council of theologians, or congress of philosophers and intellectuals. If the Bible says one thing and any man on earth says another, every truly wise man will say, *Let God be true, but every man a liar.*

Points of Difference between God and Great Men

Let me call your attention to some points on which many great men and God differ.

Existence of a Personal Devil

In the first place, many great and scholarly men differ from God regarding the existence of a personal devil. A very large number of men in our day, including some great thinkers and even some theologians of high repute, laugh at the very idea of there being any such person as the devil. Many men have said, "There is no devil but sin." And Mrs. Mary Baker Eddy, who has a great following, including many people of intelligence and culture, ridicules the idea of a personal devil. Now that is what many men say; very many men say it; many men whom you and I would be apt to listen to on many subjects say, "There is no personal devil."

What does God say? Turn in your Bible to Ephesians 6:11-12, and you will see for yourselves exactly what God says: *Put on the whole armour of God, that ye may be able to stand against the wiles of the devil. For our wrestling is not against flesh and blood, but against the principalities, against the powers, against the world-rulers of this darkness, against the spiritual hosts of wickedness in the heavenly places.*

Four verses further God says, *Withal taking up the shield of faith, wherewith ye shall be able to quench all the fiery darts of the evil one* (Ephesians 6:16). Not of evil, mind you, but *of the evil one.*

Now turn to 1 Peter 5:8 and you will see again what God says: *Be sober, be watchful: your adversary the devil, as a roaring lion, walketh about, seeking whom he may devour.* There can be no doubt about the meaning of these words by anyone who reads them with the purpose of finding out what they were intended to teach, and not merely with the purpose of distorting and twisting them to fit his own preconceived notions.

So we see that God says in the most unmistakable terms that there is a personal devil. Furthermore, God says that the devil is a being of such great cunning and great power that he is more than a match for you or me and that he is plotting our destruction, all the time working to accomplish it. Is God right about this? Or is Mrs. Eddy and the others who deny the existence of a personal devil right? God is right about it. God is always right; any man or woman who differs from God is always wrong.

When you believe that there is no devil but only your own sins, you are a sorely deceived individual; the very devil you do not think exists has deceived you, and he has done it in order to destroy you. An enemy in ambush is a particularly dangerous enemy. And a devil who has persuaded people that he does not exist at all is a particularly dangerous devil. No class of people falls so easy a prey to the devil's subtlety as the people who do not believe that there is any devil. Show me a man or woman who does not believe that there is any devil, and I will show you every time a man or woman whom the devil has blinded; he is deluding them in his work.

Future Judgment

In the second place, many men differ from God regarding a future judgment. Many men do not believe that there is to be a future judgment. Tell many men today that a time is coming when they will stand before the judgment seat of God, with His holy and all-seeing eye piercing them through and through, and that they will answer to Him for all their deeds done in the body and all their words spoken in this present life, and they will laugh at you in contempt. But what does God say? Turn to Acts 17:30-31 and read what He said through Paul to a group of Epicurean and Stoic philosophers gathered on the historic Areopagus: *Now [God] commandeth men that they should all everywhere repent: inasmuch as he hath appointed a day, in the which he will judge the world in righteousness by the man whom he hath ordained; whereof he hath given assurance unto all men, in that he hath raised him from the dead.*

Turn to Romans 14:12 and read what God says about it: *So then each one of us shall give account of himself to God.*

Turn to 2 Corinthians 5:10 and read what God says: *We must all be made manifest before the judgment-seat of Christ; that each one may receive the things done in the body, according to what he hath done, whether it be good or bad.*

Turn to Matthew 12:36 and read what God says: *I say unto you, that every idle word that men shall speak, they shall give account thereof in the day of judgment.* Can anything be plainer than God's Word on this point? Is God right or are these learned gentlemen who differ from God right? God is right, and these men who differ from God are wrong. God is always right, and men are always wrong when they differ from God. There is one thing concerning the future that is certain. It is certain that there will be a judgment day. It is not certain that you or I will live another day.

I saw a neighbor of mine walking down the street the day before yesterday. This morning, just before I came here, another neighbor came in and told me this neighbor died at ten minutes before ten last night. It is not certain that there will be another election or another Christmas; it is not certain that there will be times of peace ahead of us or times of great conflict. It is not certain what the outcome will be of the great Peace Conference being held in Washington, upon which the attention of most of the civilized world is focused. But it is certain that there will be a judgment day. It is sure that you and I will stand before the judgment seat of Christ to give account of the deeds done in the body and the words spoken in this life. It is absolutely sure that *each one of us shall give account of himself to God.*

Differences about Hell

In the third place, many men, including men who are accorded wise by the world, differ from God regarding hell. There are many today who do not believe that there will be any hell at all in the world to come. Many able and scholarly men say, "There is no hell except the hell a man makes for himself in this life, the hell of his own tormenting conscience, and the hell of troubles arising from his own misdoings."

An intelligent woman said to me a while ago, "Why, Mr. Torrey, you don't believe in hell, do you?"

It is not a question of what I believe, but of what God says. What does God say? Turn to Matthew 5:29-30: *And if thy right eye causeth thee to stumble, pluck it out, and cast it from thee: for it is profitable for thee that one of thy members should perish, and not thy whole body be cast into hell. If thy right hand causeth thee to stumble, cut it off, and cast it from thee: for it is profitable for thee that one of thy members should perish, and not thy whole body go into hell.*

Then turn to Luke 12:4-5 and read what God says: *Be not afraid of them that kill the body, and after that have no more that they can do. But I will forewarn you whom ye shall fear: Fear him, which after he hath killed hath power to cast into hell; yea, I say unto you, Fear him.*

Turn to the last book in the Bible and in Revelation chapter 21 read what God says: *But for the fearful, and unbelieving, and abominable, and murderers, and fornicators, and sorcerers, and idolaters, and all liars, their part shall be in the lake* that burneth with fire and brimstone; which is the second death* (Revelation 21:8).

Then there are many who believe that there is to be a future hell, but they do not believe it will be everlasting. Many say to me, "You don't believe in everlasting punishment, do you?" Again, I say, it is not a question of what I believe or what you believe, but of what God says.

Read Matthew 25:41: *Then shall he say also unto them on the left hand, Depart from me, ye cursed, into the eternal fire which is prepared for the devil and his angels.* Compare that with Revelation 20:10, where we are told definitely about the fire that is prepared for the devil and his angels and about its duration. This is what we read: *And the devil that deceived them was cast into the lake of fire and brimstone, where are also the beast and the false prophet* [in the next-to-the-closing verse of the preceding chapter compared with the preceding verse of this chapter, we are told that the beast and the false prophet had already been there a thousand years], *and they shall be tormented day and night for ever and ever.*

Revelation 14:9-11 says, *If any man worshippeth the beast and his image, and receiveth a mark on his forehead, or upon his hand, he also shall drink of the wine of the wrath of God, which is prepared unmixed in the cup of his anger; and he shall be tormented with fire and brimstone in the presence of the holy angels, and in the presence of the Lamb: and the smoke of their torment goeth up for ever and ever; and they have no rest day and night, they that worship the beast and his image, and whoso receiveth the mark of his name.*

Turn once more to Revelation 20:15 where we are told plainly what will come to pass at the judgment of the great white throne at the end of the millennium: *And if any was not found written in the book of life, he was cast into the lake of fire.*

Is your name written in the Book of Life? If it is not, you should speed up and get it written there today, or you will spend an endless eternity in hell. I do not state that as my own opinion; I declare it as God's word plainly set forth in His Book.

Future Probation

In the fourth place, not a few wise men, as the world counts wisdom, and not a few prominent theologians differ from God about a future probation. There are many men, often men whom the world considers very wise, who say with great confidence that if men do not repent of their sins and accept Jesus Christ now in this life, they will get another chance to repent and turn to Christ after they have died. I used to believe that myself. But what does God say?

Turn to John 8:21 and read for yourself what God says through the lips of His Son, who spoke the very words of God: *I go away, and ye shall seek me, and shall die in your sin: whither I go, ye cannot come.* Here the Lord Jesus was speaking for God; He declared in the plainest kind of language that *if men die in their sin, they cannot go where He goes.*

Turn to Hebrews 9:27 and read what God says: *It is appointed unto men once to die, but after this the judgment.* In these words, God plainly declares that what comes after death is not another probation but the judgment. If you still have any doubt as to what God says on this point, turn to 2 Corinthians 5:10: *For we must all appear before the judgment seat of Christ; that every one may receive the things done in his body, according to that he hath done, whether it be good or bad.* Here we are distinctly told that the basis of the judgment will be the *things done in [the] body,* the things done before we leave this present life, the things done while we are still in these physical body, the things done this side of the grave. And here again God is right. God is always right, and any man who differs from God is always wrong.

The Way of Salvation

In the fifth place, many men, including some of the brightest thinkers and most brilliant writers, differ from God regarding the way of salvation. Many men say that if a man lives a good moral life, he will be saved. They claim that he may be a Jew, or a Muslim, or a Buddhist, or a Christian; as long as he is sincere, he will be saved just the same. They believe no man will be lost simply because he did not believe on Jesus Christ and confess Him before the world.

When I lived in Chicago, a preacher who had a very wide reputation for his ability and claimed to be a Christian, said not long after the death of Colonel Robert Ingersoll, "Heaven or any good country will welcome a man like Colonel Ingersoll."

And the infidels applauded when he said it and exclaimed, "What a broad-minded preacher." I suppose that this professing Christian preacher was highly pleased to get the applause of the avowed enemies of Jesus Christ.

But what does God say? Turn to the words of the Lord Jesus in John 14:6: *I am the way, and the truth, and the life: no one cometh unto the Father, but by me.*

Acts 4:12 says, *Neither is there salvation in any other: for there is none other name under heaven given among men, whereby we must be saved.*

Turn to John 3:18: *He that believeth on him is not condemned: but he that believeth not is condemned already, because he hath not believed in the name of the only begotten Son of God.*

Then read John 3:36: *He that believeth on the Son hath everlasting life: and he that believeth not the Son shall not see life; but the wrath of God abideth on him.*

Turn to Romans 10:9-10: *If thou shalt confess with thy mouth the Lord Jesus, and shalt believe in thine heart that God hath raised him from the dead, thou shalt be saved. For with the heart man believeth unto righteousness; and with the mouth confession is made unto salvation.*

Turn to the words of the Lord Jesus Himself in Matthew 10:32-33: *Whosoever therefore shall confess me before men, him will I confess also before my Father which is in heaven. But whosoever shall deny me before men, him will I also deny before my Father which is in heaven.* There is no mistaking the meaning of these words by any man who desires to know what God's Word really does say.

Entering the Kingdom of God

In the sixth place, many thoughtful men, including not a few professors in Methodist and other professedly Christian colleges and universities and theological seminaries, differ from God regarding the conditions of entering into the kingdom of God. Many men say that the way to get into the kingdom of God is by leading an upright life, treating your wife and children well, being honest in business, being kind to the poor, practicing the social gospel, and on and on. Others say that the way to enter the kingdom of God is by being baptized, uniting with the church, partaking of Communion, reading the Bible, saying your prayers, going to confession, and doing other religious works. Others say that the way to enter the kingdom of God is by having a good ancestry, being carefully reared and well educated in Christian schools and colleges. But what does God say?

Turn to John 3:3-5, and you will see exactly what God says. *Jesus answered and said unto him, Verily, verily, I say unto thee, Except a man be born again, he cannot see the kingdom of God. . . . Jesus answered, Verily, verily, I say unto thee, Except a man be born of water and of the Spirit, he cannot enter into the kingdom of God.*

Then read Titus 3:5: *Not by works done in righteousness, which we did ourselves, but according to his mercy he saved us, through the washing of regeneration and renewing of the Holy [Spirit].* God says that the only way to enter the kingdom and be saved is by being born again, becoming a new creation through the power of the Holy Spirit within us.

The Time to Repent and Accept Christ

In the seventh place, many men differ from God regarding the best time to repent and accept Christ. Many of you differ from God concerning this. Many men say that there will be someday a better time than today to repent of your sins, turn to Jesus Christ, and confess Christ before the world. Many of you say it, or think it if you do not actually say it, or act it if you do not distinctly think it. But what does God say? Read 2 Corinthians 6:2: *Behold, now is the acceptable time; behold, now is the day of salvation.*

Hebrews 3:7 tells us that *the Holy [Spirit] saith, Today if ye will hear his voice.*

Read Proverbs 27:1: *Boast not thyself of tomorrow; for thou knowest not what a day may bring forth.*

Proverbs 29:1 says, *He, that being often reproved hardeneth his neck, shall suddenly be destroyed, and that without remedy.* Felix, the great Roman governor of old, thought there would be a more *convenient season* and waited for it, but he never found it. That is why he will spend eternity in hell.

These are some of the things that men say and some of the things that God says. Which will you believe? I say with Paul, *Let God be true, but every man a liar.*

But perhaps someone here will say, "But I don't believe the Bible is the Word of God." My friend, did it ever occur to you that doubting a fact does not alter the fact? Did it ever occur to you that your not believing the Bible to be the Word of God does not alter in the least the fully proven fact that the Bible is the Word of God?

At the time of the Boxer Rebellion in China, some of the Boxers did not believe they could be killed by bullets. They thought their incantations and strange rites made them invulnerable. These men were very honest and entirely sincere about this belief. A Chinese army officer demanded that they prove their sincerity by standing in line so he might have his soldiers shoot at them. They immediately consented; they were very sincere. They lined up and fearlessly faced the firing squad. The Chinese soldiers blazed away, and the Boxers dropped dead. Their doubt of the power of bullets to kill them did not alter the fact.

Your doubt that the Bible is God's Word does not alter the fact, not one iota. Suppose for a moment that the Bible turns out to be the Word of God. You must admit that there is at least a possibility that the Bible may be the Word of God. You must admit that the men and women who are really living nearest to God and know God best believe the Bible is the Word of God. Suppose they prove to be right. Where then will you be? Damned. And that is just exactly what you will be if you go on doubting God's Word and rejecting God's Son, listening to the voice of men rather than to the voice of God.

God says that there is a devil and that you need Christ's help against his cunning and power. God says that there is a future judgment and that we must all appear before the judgment seat of Christ to receive the things done in the body. God says that there is a hell and that it is a place of torment where all who reject Christ in this life will spend eternity. God says that there is no future probation, that the issues of eternity are settled in this life. God says that there is only one way to be saved – by accepting Jesus Christ as our Savior, surrendering ourselves to Him as our Lord, and confessing Him as such before the world. God says that the only way to enter the kingdom of God is by being born again by the power of the Holy Spirit and accepting the Lord Jesus Christ. God says that the best time to accept Christ and to be saved is right now.

Behold, now is the acceptable time (2 Corinthians 6:2).

The Holy [Spirit] sayeth, Today (Hebrews 3:7).

Boast not thyself of tomorrow; for thou knowest not what a day may bring forth (Proverbs 27:1).

He, that being often reproved hardeneth his neck, shall suddenly be destroyed, and that without remedy (Proverbs 29:1).

Who will turn from sin and unbelief and turn to Christ right now?

Reuben A. Torrey – A Brief Biography

Reuben A. Torrey was an author, conference speaker, pastor, evangelist, Bible college dean, and more. Reuben Archer Torrey was born in Hoboken, New Jersey, on January 28, 1856. He graduated from Yale University in 1875 and from Yale Divinity School in 1878, when he became the pastor of a Congregational church in Garrettsville, Ohio. Torrey married Clara Smith in 1879, with whom he had five children.

In 1882, he went to Germany, where he studied at the universities at Leipzig and Erlangen. Upon returning to the United States, R. A. Torrey pastored in Minneapolis, and was also in charge of the Congregational City Mission Society. In 1889, D. L. Moody called upon Torrey to lead his Chicago Evangelization Society, which later became the Moody Bible Institute. Beginning in 1894, Torrey was also the pastor of the Chicago Avenue Church, which was later called the Moody Memorial Church. He was a chaplain with the YMCA during the Spanish-American War, and was also a chaplain during World War I.

Torrey traveled all over the world leading evangelistic tours, preaching to the unsaved. It is believed that more than one hundred thousand were saved under his preaching. In 1908, he helped start the Montrose Bible Conference in Pennsylvania, which continues today. He became dean of the Bible Institute of Los Angeles (now Biola University) in 1912, and was the pastor of the Church of the Open Door in Los Angeles from 1915 to 1924.

Torrey continued speaking all over the world and holding Bible conferences. He died in Asheville, North Carolina, on October 26, 1928.

R. A. Torrey was a very active evangelist and soul winner, speaking to people everywhere he went, in public and in private, about their souls, seeking to lead the lost to Jesus. He authored more than forty books, including *How to Bring Men to Christ*, *How to Pray*, *How to Study the Bible for Greatest Profit*, *How to Obtain Fullness of Power in Christian Life and Service*, and *Why God Used D. L. Moody*, and also helped edit the twelve-volume book about the fundamentals of the faith, titled *The Fundamentals*. He was also known as a man of prayer, and his teaching, preaching, writing, and his entire life proved that he walked closely with God.

Other Similar Titles

Jesus Came to Save Sinners, by Charles H. Spurgeon

This is a heart-level conversation with you, the reader. Every excuse, reason, and roadblock for not coming to Christ is examined and duly dealt with. If you think you may be too bad, or if perhaps you really are bad and you sin either openly or behind closed doors, you will discover that life in Christ is for you too. You can reject the message of salvation by faith, or you can choose to live a life of sin after professing faith in Christ, but you cannot change the truth as it is, either for yourself or for others. As such, it behooves you and your family to embrace truth, claim it for your own, and be genuinely set free for now and eternity. Come and embrace this free gift of God, and live a victorious life for Him.

Available where books are sold.

The Way to God, by Dwight L. Moody

There is life in Christ. Rich, joyous, wonderful life. It is true that the Lord disciplines those whom He loves and that we are often tempted by the world and our enemy, the devil. But if we know how to go beyond that temptation to cling to the cross of Jesus Christ and keep our eyes on our Lord, our reward both here on earth and in heaven will be 100 times better than what this world has to offer.

This book is thorough. It brings to life the love of God, examines the state of the unsaved individual's soul, and analyzes what took place on the cross for our sins. *The Way to God* takes an honest look at our need to repent and follow Jesus, and gives hope for unending, joyous eternity in heaven.

Available where books are sold.

How to Study the Bible Intentionally, by Reuben A Torrey

Nothing is more important for our own mental, moral, and spiritual development, or for our increase in usefulness, than Bible study. But, not all Bible study is equally profitable. Some Bible study is absolutely profitless. How to study the Bible so as to get the most benefit from it is a topic of immeasurable importance.

The practicality and effectiveness of these Bible study methods and conditions have been tested in the classroom, and not with classes made up completely of college graduates, but largely composed of people of very simple education. The methods, however, require time and hard work. It must be remembered that the Bible contains gold, and almost anyone is willing to dig for gold, especially if it is certain that he will find it. It is certain that one will find gold in the Bible – if he digs. As you use the methods recommended in this book, you will find your ability to do the work rapidly increasing by exercise, until you can soon do more in fifteen minutes than you could do in an hour when you started.

Available where books are sold.

How to Succeed in the Christian Life, by Reuben A Torrey

"I have for years felt the need of a book to put in the hands of those beginning the Christian life that would tell them just how to make a complete success of this new life upon which they were entering. I could find no such book, so I have been driven to write one. This book aims to tell the young convert just what he most needs to know. I hope that pastors and evangelists and other Christian workers may find it a good book to put in the hands of young converts. I hope that it may also prove a helpful book to many who have long been Christians but have not made that headway in the Christian life that they long for."

– Reuben A. Torrey

Available where books are sold.

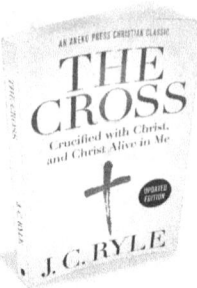

The Cross, by John C. Ryle

I want to tell you what perhaps the greatest Christian who ever lived (the Apostle Paul) thought of the cross of Christ. Believe me, the cross is of deepest importance. This is no mere question of controversy; this is not one of those points on which men may agree to differ and feel that differences will not shut them out of heaven. A man must be right on this subject, or he is lost forever. Heaven or hell, happiness or misery, life or death, blessing or cursing in the last day – all hinges on the answer to this question: "What do you think about the cross of Christ?"

Available where books are sold.

Repentance, by John C. Ryle

It is indifference that leaves people alone and allows them to go their own way. It is love, tender love, that warns them and raises the cry of alarm. The cry of "Fire! Fire!" at midnight might sometimes rudely, harshly, and unpleasantly startle a person out of his sleep, but who would complain if that cry was the means of saving his life? The words Except you repent, you will all likewise perish might at first seem stern and severe, but they are words of love, and they could be the means of delivering precious souls from hell.

Available where books are sold.

How to Study the Bible, by Dwight L. Moody

There is no situation in life for which you cannot find some word of consolation in Scripture. If you are in affliction, if you are in adversity and trial, there is a promise for you. In joy and sorrow, in health and in sickness, in poverty and in riches, in every condition of life, God has a promise stored up in His Word for you.

This classic book by Dwight L. Moody brings to light the necessity of studying the Scriptures, presents methods which help stimulate excitement for the Scriptures, and offers tools to help you comprehend the difficult passages in the Scriptures. To live a victorious Christian life, you must read and understand what God is saying to you. Moody is a master of using stories to illustrate what he is saying, and you will be both inspired and convicted to pursue truth from the pages of God's Word.

Available where books are sold.

The Kneeling Christian, by Albert Richardson

The Lord Jesus is as powerful today as ever before. The Lord Jesus is as anxious for men to be saved as ever before. His arm is not shortened that it cannot save, but He does stretch forth His arm unless we pray more – and more genuinely. Prayer, real prayer, is the noblest, the sublimest and most stupendous act that any creature of God can perform. Lord, teach us how to pray.

Available where books are sold.

Life in Christ, by Charles H. Spurgeon

Men who were led by the hand or groped their way along the wall to reach Jesus were touched by his finger and went home without a guide, rejoicing that Jesus Christ had opened their eyes. Jesus is still able to perform such miracles. And, with the power of the Holy Spirit, his Word will be expounded and we'll watch for the signs to follow, expecting to see them at once. Why shouldn't those who read this be blessed with the light of heaven? This is my heart's inmost desire.

I can't put fine words together. I've never studied speech. In fact, my heart loathes the very thought of intentionally speaking with fine words when souls are in danger of eternal separation from God. No, I work to speak straight to your hearts and consciences, and if there is anyone with faith to receive, God will bless them with fresh revelation.

Available where books are sold.

Pilgrim's Progress, by John Bunyan

Often disguised as something that would help him, evil accompanies Christian on his journey to the Celestial City. As you walk with him, you'll begin to identify today's many religious pitfalls. These are presented by men such as Pliable, who turns back at the Slough of Despond; and Ignorance, who believes he's a true follower of Christ when he's really only trusting in himself. Each character represented in this allegory is intentionally and profoundly accurate in its depiction of what we see all around us, and unfortunately, what we too often see in ourselves. But while Christian is injured and nearly killed, he eventually prevails to the end. So can you.

Available where books are sold.

www.ingramcontent.com/pod-product-compliance
Lightning Source LLC
Chambersburg PA
CBHW070137080526
44586CB00015B/1735